Life Happens

Get

Ready

BARRY ST. CLAIR

BROADMAN
&HOLMAN
PUBLISHERS

Nashville, Tennessee

Published by Broadman & Holman Publishers, Nashville, Tennessee
Acquisitions & Development Editor: Janis Whipple
Interior Design: Desktop Miracles, Addison, Texas
Published in association with the literary agency of Alive Communications, Inc.,
1465 Kelly Johnson Blvd., Suite 320, Colorado Springs, CO 80920.

4262-94
0-8054-6294-5

Dewey Decimal Classification: 248.83
Subject Heading: CHRISTIAN LIFE / TEENAGERS—RELIGIOUS LIFE
Library of Congress Card Catalog Number: 96-41905

Unless otherwise noted, Scripture quotations are from the Holy Bible, New International Version, copyright © 1973, 1978, 1984 by International Bible Society. Other Scripture are marked NASB, the New American Standard Bible, © the Lockman Foundation, 1960, 1962, 1963, 1968, 1971, 1972, 1973, 1975, 1977, used by permission; NRSV, New Revised Standard Version of the Bible, copyright © 1989 by the Division of Christian Education of the National Council of Churches of Christ in the United States of America, used by permission, all rights reserved; RSV, Revised Standard Version of the Bible, copyrighted 1946, 1952, © 1971, 1973; TLB, The Living Bible, copyright © Tyndale House Publishers, Wheaton, Ill., 1971, used by permission; THE MESSAGE, the New Testament in Contemporary English, © 1993 by Eugene H. Peterson, published by NavPress, Colorado Springs, Colo.

Library of Congress Cataloging-in-Publication Data

St. Clair, Barry
    Life happens : get ready / Barry St. Clair
        p. cm.
    Includes bibliographical references.
    ISBN 0-8054-6294-5 (pbk.)
    1. Teenagers—Religious life. 2. Teenagers—Conduct of life. I. Title.
BV4531.2.S674   1997
248.8'45—dc20   96-41905
                                                                                          CIP

99 00 01 5

In honor of my parents,
Howard and Kitty St. Clair,
I write this book.

WITH LOVE THEY ENCOURAGED ME to pursue my destiny. Because of them I never doubted that it was special.

From my dad I learned to dream big dreams and then pursue them. From my mom I learned to persevere through the tough times. From them both I learned to turn to the Lord.

They pursued God's special destiny for them in their generation, and they have left me a legacy that has positively encouraged me to pursue God's unique destiny for me in my generation.

And now Carol and I have the privilege of doing the same with our children and they in turn with their children —generation to generation until all know that God has a destiny for them.

Thanks, Mom and Dad, for leaving me a legacy that pointed to God's destiny for me!

You have made known to me
the path of life;
you will fill me with joy
in your presence,
with eternal pleasures
at your right hand.

PSALM 16:11

THE TEAM EFFORT ON THIS BOOK made it possible. Jody Graham, thanks for your encouragement to put what I spoke into print. Beth Wilson and Mark Deaton, I appreciate you for typing my notes and helping me in so many other ways. To my office staff who covered for me when I was hiding out, especially Susan Nichols and Brad Leeper. Most of all, thanks to my Carol, who loves me in spite of myself, who never gives up on me, who has sacrificed many hours of time with me so I could complete this project, and who always encourages me to pursue my dreams.

REACH OUT MINISTRIES
Equipping for Strategic Youth Ministry
3961 Holcomb Bridge Road
Suite 201
Norcross, GA 30092

Phone: 770-441-2247
Fax: 770-449-7544
Email: 72002.1704@compuserve.com

Psalm 139.

Conten**t**s

Acknowledgments iv
What's the Big Deal about This Book? vii
How to Max Out This Book ix

WHERE AM I GOING?

1. Let's Party 2
    What is your destiny,
    and how can you get in on it?
2. Open the Presents 10
    What spiritual resources do you have,
    and what do you do with them?
3. Take a Trip 18
    What is your destination,
    and how are you going to get there?
4. Look for the Billboards 24
    How can you get where you are going
    and not give up on the way?

WHO AM I?

5. Vote for Yourself 32
    What is your personality,
    and how can you enjoy it?
6. Pull Out the Credit Card 47
    What are your spiritual gifts,
    and how can you use them?
7. Go for the Best 59
    What are your abilities and experiences,
    and how can you maximize them?
8. Give It All 71
    What motivates you,
    and how do you give 100 percent?

HOW AM I GOING TO GET THERE?

9. Aim at the Target 84
   What is your life purpose,
   and how do you discover it?
10. Know Which End Is Up 91
    What are your values,
    and how do you define them?
11. Run for the Finish Line 99
    What are your goals,
    and how do you reach them?
12. Watch the Clock 107
    What time do you have,
    and how do you use it?
13. Warp and Weft 'Em 116
    What decisions do you need to make,
    and how do you make them?
14. Put Together "The Visible Man" 124
    What is integrity,
    and how do you pursue it?

Notes 133

What's the Big Deal about This Book?

YOU ARE!

I know that deciding what to do this Saturday is a long-range plan for most of us. But also I know that the "biggies" will be decided in the next five years.

Where will you be in five years?
What school will you attend?
Who will you have as friends?
Who will you be dating?
Who will your husband or wife be?
(Scary thoughts!)

The "biggies" will be determined by deciding your future now.

Who is Jesus Christ to you?
What kind of personality do you have?
What spiritual gifts do you possess?
What motivates you?
What is your purpose in life?
What do you value?
What are your goals?
How do you make decisions?

Answering these questions now will *protect* you from wasting your life and *provide* you with the resources to fulfill your unique and special destiny.

Lloyd's Bank of London followed 100,000 paper clips and observed that only about 2,000 were used to hold papers together. The bank said:

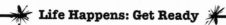

- 14,163 others were bent and twisted during telephone conversations.
- 19,143 were used as chips in card games.
- 7,200 clipped together garments.
- 5,434 became toothpicks or ear scratchers.
- 5,308 were converted into nail cleaners.
- 3,916 cleaned pipes.

The rest, about 25,000, fell ingloriously to the floor and were swept away.

How could something so neatly invented and so useful be so misused and, often, at least, seemingly wasted? You want to ask yourself that question about your life. Are you picking teeth and cleaning nails when clearly God has made you for something much more?

How to Max Out This Book

THIS BOOK CAN CHANGE YOU TOTALLY! It will help you answer three important questions:

Where am I going?
  Who am I?
    How am I going to get there?

Because the answers to those questions are so important, I want you to get the most out of this book.

Most students today are grossly underchallenged. What you discover here will change that. In it you will discover your destiny. Your destiny is that unique purpose for which God created you—both now and in the future. He has a very special plan designed only for you. As you find His design, you will be motivated to pursue it with a passion!

So how do you max out this book?

- *Pray* before each session. This prayer would be a good one: "Lord, help me discover something new about You and me."

- *Work* through the chapter.
  - Read the material.
  - Look up the Bible verses.
  - Think through your answers.
  - Write down the answers.
  - Jot down any questions you have.

- *Focus* on the "Get Ready" section. It will help you to see how what you are learning fits into your life.
  - Set aside at least half an hour to work on this.
  - Take your time.
  - Think and pray about it. Let God show you who you are.

- *Apply* what you discover that week. Answer the question:

"This week how will I use what I learned?"

- *Talk* about what you learned with one of your parents or with friends.
    —I wrote a book for your parents so they can help you with this.
    —Take time to sit down with them and discuss the things you are thinking. In my opinion this is the ideal way to get the most out of this book.
    —Your youth leader may want to get some groups going through the book. That is another opportunity to discuss what you are learning.
    —You can ask a friend or an accountability/prayer partner to go through it with you. Meet together each week to talk about what you are discovering.

- *Lead* someone else through the book after you have finished. Invite a friend or group of friends to read the book and meet with you to discuss it.

Life happens! It's time for you to *get ready!*

chapter 1

Let's Party

What is your destiny, and how can you get in on it?

Sweet Sixteen! My daughter Katie got breakfast in bed. Immediately after school I took Katie to get her driver's license. She drove out of there without hitting one parallel parking cone and with her license. And we made it home without a wreck!

That night, seven friends arrived to celebrate. And celebrate we did! We drove across Atlanta to the $3 Cafe. (Not as cheap as it sounds!) We ate burgers and drank cokes and watched movie clips on a large screen TV. Then we drove down to see Steve McCoy, DJ for "Star 94." He had taken the challenge to stay up on an Atlanta Braves billboard until the Braves won the pennant. He came down to talk and to wish Katie a happy birthday. Big night!

Describe your greatest birthday ever.

_____

_____

_____

Why was it so special?

_____

_____

_____

Physical birth, spiritual birth—both are worth celebrating because both show how special we are. In both we begin the journey toward our true destiny, the specific purpose for which God created us.

So let's sing "Happy Birthday!" Let's discover our destiny! Let's party!

CATCHING A GORGEOUS GLIMPSE

When I visit my folks in West Virginia, I have a route that I jog out on Old Ingleside Road. I run up the mountain, turn along the ridge to Mt. Horeb Church, and then return. On this particular day it had just stopped raining. As I ran along the ridge I looked to my right just as the sun burst through the clouds. When it headed down over the edge of the mountain, reflecting against the leaves, the brilliancy of the gold, red, and orange was incredible. It stopped me in my tracks. I said out loud, "Lord, that is unbelievably gorgeous. Thank You for letting me get a little glimpse of You."

We have that same sense of awe when we begin to discover our destiny. When we see God's gorgeous picture of who He is, what He is like, and what He has done for us, then that changes everything. That understanding changes especially the way we see ourselves and the way we see the future God has for us.

That gorgeous glimpse of our destiny resounds in the words of the apostle Paul.

Because of the sacrifice of the Messiah, his blood poured out on the altar of the Cross, we're a free people—free of penalties and punishments chalked up by all our misdeeds. And not just barely free, either. *Abundantly free!* He thought of everything, provided for everything we could possibly need, letting us in on the plans he took such delight in making. He set it all out before us in Christ, a long-range plan in which everything would be brought together and summed up in him, everything in deepest heaven, everything on planet earth.

It's in Christ that we find out who we are and what we are living for. Long before we first heard of Christ and got our hopes up, he had his eye on us, had designs on us for glorious living, part of the overall purpose he is working out in everything and everyone. (Eph. 1:9–12, THE MESSAGE)

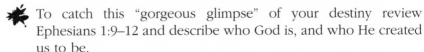 To catch this "gorgeous glimpse" of your destiny review Ephesians 1:9–12 and describe who God is, and who He created us to be.

_____

_____

_____

| We were created to live "in Christ." He is our destiny. |

Wow! With great delight God eagerly wants to show us our destiny. He centered our destiny around Jesus Christ. We were created to live "in Christ." When we live "in Christ," much more than only pursuing our future life direction is involved—we discover who He is. He is our destiny.

 Read Ephesians 1:1–14 and circle the phrases "in Christ," "in him," and "in the One he loves." Count them. How many times do those phrases occur?

God wants us to know that our destiny is "in Christ." But what does that mean?

BACK TO THE FUTURE

Being "in Christ" is somewhat like getting into Dr. Emmett Brown's DeLorean in *Back to the Future.* To get in the time machine and go all the way back to our future "in Christ" is wilder than Marty McFly dating his own mother! Let's hop in and take a ride.

The Past

The Mess Up. From a perfect life to the pits, people made a mess out of God's destiny.

Describe what happened that messed up your destiny before you even arrived on the scene.

Genesis 3:6–13

_____

_____

_____

_____

_____

_____

_____

_____

_____

_____

This created a gigantic gulf between God and the rest of His creation. Throughout the Old Testament people tried to find a way back to their destiny, to bridge the gulf between themselves and God. Men and women made laws, offered sacrifices, worshiped idols, and tried doing their own thing—none of which worked.

- How have you tried to do that in your life?

_____

_____

_____

The Fix Up. These futile attempts to discover their destiny continued until Jesus was born.

✴ Discover what Jesus did to restore your hope for the future in Galatians 4:4–5.

_____

_____

_____

Jesus went into the blackness of separation from God. He plunged into the gulf until the darkness caused Him to cry out, "My God, my God, why have you forsaken me?" While Satan and the human wickedness did their worst, He endured the cross. Then came the great cry, "It is finished." Now, no rift, no gulf. He pulled it all back together. His was a rescue mission—to redeem us who had been kidnapped. He is the "first-born of all creation"— the ultimate of what human beings can become. Jesus gave us another shot at our destiny.

> **Jesus gave us**
>
> **another shot**
>
> **at our destiny.**

✴ What does that mean to you?

_____

_____

_____

The Present

The Struggle. Maybe you thought you had to reach your destiny on your own power. For a long time I tried to live the Christian life like the guys I took on a canoe trip.

> The vehicles took us to the end of the road in the Maine woods. The counselors took the canoes off the racks and put three junior high kids under each one to carry them to the water. Three scrawny guys, who already had backpacks and supplies to carry, hauled these canoes over their heads. It would have been one thing to have carried them one hundred yards, but they kept going . . . and going . . . and going. Unlike the Energizer Bunny, they got real tired, real fast. Sweating profusely from carrying the heavy canoes, the hot day, and walking so far, one stumbled over a root. The canoe lurched forward. It rammed the canoe ahead, causing it to ram the next one. Kids, canoes, paddles, and gear were scattered all over the trail.
>
> Finally they got to the river. They let out a "wahoo" when they dropped the canoes in the water. We put the gear on board, got all the guys in, pushed out into the current, and "chilled." The scenery wasn't much different than when we were walking in the woods, but it sure was a lot more enjoyable.

This story illustrates what it means to be "out of Christ." Many people struggle through life carrying the canoe over their heads, exerting incredible effort to get where they're going. The result is exhaustion, frustration, and lives strewn along the trail.

How much better to put the canoe "in (the river of) Christ" and let Him carry you.

Describe one time in your life when you struggled "outside of Christ."

_____

_____

_____

Describe one time when you flowed down the river of life "in Christ."

_____

_____

_____

The Triangle. Let's visualize ourselves as a triangle. Each side represents a different, but important, aspect of who we are.

In the area of *relationships,* we may have many friends and a great family, but somewhere along the way someone is going to let us down. Having a friend reject us, dealing with breaking up with a boyfriend or girlfriend, feeling the pain parents' can inflict—any of these can cause that side of the triangle to collapse.

In the area of *skills,* we may have many talents and abilities; but no matter how talented we are, someone—somewhere—is going to be better than we are. Failing a test, getting injured playing ball, getting fired from a job—all of these and many other circumstances can cause us to question our abilities.

That is why it's so important to build our self-image on the base of the triangle: *self-worth.* Self-worth is based on who we are on the inside, who Christ is in us.

The Prayer. Now, in this present time, each of us can enter into our destiny. We can do that by placing ourselves "in Christ." We place ourselves "in Christ" by sincerely saying to Him,

> *"Jesus, I open up my life to You. I turn from myself and my sin. I invite You to come and take control of my life."*

When any person "opens the door" of his or her life, Jesus will come in (Revelation 3:20). At that point a person is "in Christ." It is life's most important decision! You can make it right now if you have not done so before.

If you have received Christ already, affirm that in a prayer.

✳ Write out the prayer above in your own words.

_____

_____

_____

 Say this out loud to yourself.

> When Christ died, I died.
> When Christ rose, I rose.
> I am in Christ.
> Christ is in me.
> Now I have a changed identity.

The Future

One day, out there in the future, God is going to bring back together everything that sin and Satan have tried to destroy.

❋ According to Ephesians 1:9–10, what is God going to do?

_____

_____

_____

❋ From Philippians 2:9–11 outline how that is going to happen.

_____

_____

_____

Picture a scoreboard. On one side you have the home team's score; on the other you have your opponent's score. Whoever has a higher score at the end of the game wins. The loser cries. The winner celebrates.

In the same way, one day in the future everyone will bow before Jesus as Lord. Some will have placed themselves on the losers' side by living their lives outside of Christ, and they will be heartbroken. Others will have placed themselves "in Christ," and they will celebrate.

❋ Where will you be? Why?

_____

_____

_____

> **Self-worth is based on who we are on the inside, who Christ is in us.**

Just as Katie's sixteenth birthday celebrated a rite of passage into adulthood, in the same way our spiritual birth is our rite of passage into the incredible depths of who we are in Christ—past, present, and future. More than a formal religious exercise or an emotional experience that passes after a few weeks, it determines who we are. Placing our lives "in Christ" decides our destiny for eternity.

GET READY

- If, as you read this chapter, you sensed that you have never placed your life "in Christ," you can do that now. If you prayed the prayer earlier, affirm that decision by thanking God that you are now "in Christ." Write out your prayer here.

_____

_____

_____

- Celebrate your own birthday! From your discovery in this chapter, describe in three sentences what it means to you to be "in Christ."

#1 _____

_____

_____

#2 _____

_____

_____

#3 _____

_____

_____

- Express what you think your destiny is.

_____

_____

_____

- Name two people you will tell what you learned this week (1 parent, 1 friend):

1. _____

2. _____

Ask them if you can tell them what you are learning every week. If you are in a group, that's excellent. Even better: talk to one of your parents about your discoveries each week.

chapter 2. Open the Presents

What spiritual resources do you have, and what can you do with them?

As a part of Katie's sixteenth birthday, I took her out to a fancy restaurant. The thirty-ninth floor revolved offering a panoramic view of Atlanta. After a delicious meal and relaxed conversation, I pulled a small, gift-wrapped box out of my pocket. I told Katie that her mother and I had selected this with special care. She opened it to discover a ruby ring. With it I had attached a note: "You are worth far more than rubies (Proverbs 31:10)! We love you. Mom and Dad."

THAT PRESENT EXPRESSED TO KATIE her worth to us.

✳ What is the best gift someone has ever given you?

_____

_____

_____

Better than the best gifts we have ever received are the ones we possess when we place ourselves "in Christ." Check them out. Open them up. Not only do they show you how special you are to your heavenly Father; they also provide the spiritual resources you need to move toward your destiny.

PRESENT #1—BLESSINGS

✳ Looking at Ephesians 1:3, what blessings has God given you?

_____

_____

_____

Lena translates for me when I travel to the Ukraine. Her father works two jobs for a total salary of twenty-four dollars a month. Her family has never eaten at a restaurant. She used the forty-five dollars I gave her to buy a warm winter coat for her mile-and-a-half walk every day to catch the train to and from school. Yet she has joy, peace, and unbelievable patience in the midst of an economic system that doesn't work. Lena has ripped open the present of "spiritual blessings."

"Some things a person can work for or discover on his own—certain skills, position, or wealth. But other things are beyond his ability to attain—goodness, humility or peace of mind. 'Spiritual blessings' are those blessings that only God can give."[1]

Those blessings belong to us, as believers. What spiritual blessings do you need from God right now?

_____

_____

_____

PRESENT #2—CHOSEN

Let's unwrap the next present in Ephesians 1:4. What is it?

_____

_____

_____

Since the stars have hung in space which some say could be billions of years, God has had us in His plans for at least that long! He chose us "before the foundation of the world."

He chose us "to be holy and blameless in his sight." Are you holy? Are you blameless?

_____

_____

_____

Imagine your whole life laid out on one of those slides you used in biology class. Placed under the microscope, what does God see? All the things you have done wrong? Your mistakes? Your

> **All God sees when He looks at you is Jesus Christ!**

messed up relationships? No! All He sees when He looks at you is Jesus Christ!

"That doesn't make sense; I sin a lot" you say. Because you are "in Christ," God doesn't look at that. All He sees is Jesus, holy and blameless in you. Every day He is working to change your attitudes and actions to reflect that. You are becoming who you already are!

In what ways do you need to see yourself as holy and blameless?

_____

_____

_____

PRESENT #3—ADOPTION

God had only one Son. Everyone else who belongs to Him is adopted.

How does the apostle Paul explain that in Ephesians 1:5?

_____

_____

_____

In the Roman Empire adoption had special significance. The person to be adopted, often out of slavery, went through a ritual of being sold and bought back twice. The third time the person was sold and *not* bought back. Then the adoptive parents signed the papers to legalize the adoption. Finally, the adopted person verbally surrendered all rights of the old family and slavery and took on all the rights of his or her new family and freedom.

Similarly God has adopted us into His family. Describe how that works from John 1:12.

_____

_____

_____

As God's children we have many privileges. For one, — God "our Father." In fact, Jesus encourages us to use the e. term "Abba," which means "daddy." In a world where good i. are in short supply, it's wonderful to have the perfect Father. If yc relationship with your father is less than the best, then having this kind of relationship with your heavenly Father can fill in the gaps. If you struggle with even thinking about God as a Father, I encourage you to imagine yourself sitting on His lap, snuggling up to Him, and letting Him put His arms around you. Let your Father love you.

Ask your Father to tell you what he thinks of you. Write what you think He is saying to you.

_____

_____

_____

Becoming part of a family means we become heirs. (Romans 8:17). All of the resources Jesus possessed, we possess now. What are those resources?

- 1 John 4:19_____
- Ephesians 1:7_____
- Galatians 3:13, 1 Peter 1:18 _____
- 2 Corinthians 5:17 _____
- 1 Peter 1:15–16 _____
- John 8:32 _____
- Ephesians 1:6_____
- Philippians 4:13_____
- Acts 1:8_____
- Colossians 2:3 _____

Now we can pursue our destiny knowing what a special family we have!

Present #4—Redemption

If a kidnapper took one of your family members, how would you react? How would you feel? How much would you pay to get that person back?

_____

_____

_____

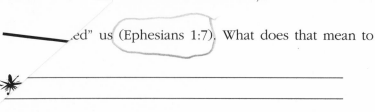

ed" us (Ephesians 1:7). What does that mean to

_____

_____

_____

Picture a slave market. Chains bind the slaves. Some benevolent benefactor, offering a large sum of money, buys the slave, removing the chains and setting him free.

We had been kidnapped by Satan. We were slaves to sin and selfishness. But Jesus came into the slave market to buy us back, and He took us out of the slave market forever.

 According to 1 Peter 1:18–19, what did it cost Him?

_____

_____

You may say, "I've done some pretty rotten things in my life, and I don't think God can forgive me." Go a step further. Imagine some things even worse than what you have done. Think of the worst crime you could commit. How much forgiveness would you need to take care of it?

Our family loved to eat at Mother Tucker's. They featured a sixty-dish salad bar, prime rib, a vegetable bar, spareribs on a sideboard, bread, apple dumplings for dessert, and seconds on everything. I would pig out! No matter how much I ate, they always had more.

God's forgiveness comes in quantities like that. He "lavished" it on us (Ephesians 1:8). How much forgiveness do you need? If you only need a little, then He will give a little. If you need more, He will give more. If you need mega, He lavishes mega-forgiveness on you. He has taken away all of our sin with mega-forgiveness at the cross. He bought us back with the price of His own blood!

Now nothing from our past holds us back. Destiny here we come!

PRESENT #5—GOD'S PLAN

When we play "Charades," we try to figure out the movie, book, or TV program the other team has written down. Without talking we give gestures that are clues to help the team guess the answer. When

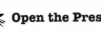

the person starts acting, then everybody on that team yells their guesses until someone gets it or time expires.

People want to know, "What is God's plan for me?" Is it a guessing game? No way. "He made known to us the mystery of his will" (Ephesians 1:9). "In Christ" He took all the guesswork out of our future.

What major clues has God given us in Ephesians 1:9–10?

_____

_____

_____

If we desire to know God's plan, we must bring every decision, dream, desire, goal, and relationship "under one head, even Christ" (Ephesians 1:10). We answer "Yes, Lord," no matter what the question. What areas of your life do you need to bring "under Christ" and say "Yes, Lord"?

_____

_____

_____

PRESENT #6—ACCEPTANCE

Being included is a wonderful thing.

> My friend Dave Busby had polio and cystic fibrosis as a boy. Since he was always sick, athletics was not his thing. But his older brother had athletic talent. When friends came over to play, Dave would dribble the ball off his gimpy legs. One Saturday morning when he was shooting around with all of his brother's friends, they made fun of him. When it came time to choose sides, he wasn't afraid he would be chosen last; he didn't think he would be chosen at all. His brother was one of the captains. He had first choice. He pointed at his little brother and said, "I choose you, Dave." That made such a profound impact on Dave's life that even now as an adult his view of God is colored by having been included by his brother.

God includes us like that. How did He express it in Ephesians 1:13?

_____

_____

_____

Like Dave, we aren't included for our abilities, talents or performance, but because we have an Older Brother.

Many people try to work hard to gain approval from family or friends. They feel they have to meet certain performance standards to be included.

- If I achieve success . . .
- If I get good grades . . .
- If I lose weight . . .
- If I make money . . .
- If I go to church . . .

This leads to fear of failure and perfectionistic tendencies. If this goes on long enough and we get rejected enough, it will cause high levels of anxiety and deep depression.

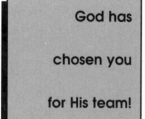

God has

chosen you

for His team!

Only one solution exists to combat this fear and anxiety: total, absolute, unconditional acceptance. Jesus is the only One who accepts you like that. When you placed yourself "in Christ," you stepped off the performance treadmill and you stepped into the friendship of One who knows everything about you—good and bad—and still He chooses you for His team. Pursuing your destiny becomes so much more relaxed when we know we are included on the team and will never be cut.

PRESENT #7—THE HOLY SPIRIT

Did you ever have a letter-writing romance? Guys don't tend to do this well, but girls sure do. When I got one of those letters, no one had to announce its arrival. Everyone could tell by the smell! It reeked of perfume. I don't know which part of the letter I enjoyed more—reading it or smelling it. Before I opened it, one mark on the letter would get me fired up, and it wasn't the postmark. The letter was sealed with a kiss!

✳ When we were marked "in Christ," we were sealed with a "kiss." According to Ephesians 1:13, what was that "kiss"?

_____

_____

_____

The Holy Spirit makes sure we get every other gift that God has for us. And there are a bundle of them—character, integrity, love, boldness, sensitivity, power, and communication, to name a few.

Can you fulfill your destiny? Not without the Holy Spirit. How would you express a prayer asking Him to release His presence and power in you so you can be and do all He intended?

_____

_____

_____

That ring I gave Katie was a very special present. She wears it with pride. But how small and insignificant it was compared to any one of these presents God has given us "in Christ." With all of these opened presents we have all we will ever need to fulfill God's destiny. Let's put the rings on our fingers and wear them!

GET READY

Think about what you face at home, at school, and with your friends, and relate one specific, practical way you will use each of the seven "presents" in the next week.

1. Blessings _____

2. Chosen _____

3. Adoption _____

4. Redemption _____

5. God's Will _____

6. Acceptance _____

7. Holy Spirit _____

chapter 3

Take a Trip

What is your destination, and how are you going to get there?

When I was growing up, my dad liked to take shortcuts on family trips.

"Where are we headed, Dad?"

"Don't worry. We're taking a shortcut."

Every time we got lost. Mom would suggest that we stop and get directions.

"No, I'm sure we are headed in the right direction."

An hour later we would discover that for the last two hours we had been making a beeline to Disney World. But our destination was Washington, D.C.!

IT'S SOMETHING ABOUT DADS. I do exactly the same thing with my family.

Our family knew who we were, but we got confused on our directions. In the same way, we can know our destiny and still get confused about how to arrive at our destination.

DON'T TAKE A WRONG TURN

We can make a wrong turn by viewing God and His plan incorrectly. If we view God as the Celestial Scrooge sitting in heaven with His fifty-pound King James Bible and a big stick, then it's hard to want to follow His plan. Often we think of our future in the following narrow, negative terms:

- A needle in a haystack. We must constantly search for our destination. Now and then God whispers, "You're getting warmer."
- A wasted life. If we pursue what God wants, then He will send us to "Bogabogaland" and ruin our lives.
- A tightrope. If we make one wrong move, one bad decision, then we will fall off the tightrope and destroy the rest of our lives.
- A computer printout. The "Big Computer in the Sky" will lay out every specific, detailed step of God's will for the rest of

our lives. We can't leave home without it. If we do, we will never know God's plan.

 In what ways have you thought about your future in these, or other, negative terms?

_____

_____

_____

To recognize these possible wrong turns before we begin the trip will keep us from wasting time in getting to our destination and keep us on the right road on the way there.

Straight Ahead

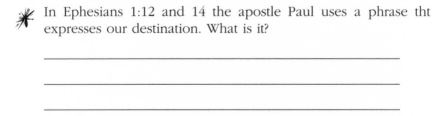

The flight took me from Kansas City to Chicago, then to Winnipeg, and on to Regina, Canada. From there the van drove an hour and a half down a highway through the wheat fields of western Canada. At one point the van driver pointed down the road and said, "Do you see that blue spot out in the distance?" I could see it easily. Not one building or tree stood between us and that blue roof. He said, "That is where we are going." It took us twenty minutes to get there! That is how far down the road we could see.

God's destination for us is like that. It is way off in the distance, but it is possible to see it and experience it now. Look out in the distance. You can see it.

 In Ephesians 1:12 and 14 the apostle Paul uses a phrase tht expresses our destination. What is it?

_____

_____

_____

Our Destination Is Future!

When the apostle Paul used these phrases, he definitely had the future in mind.

 Look at Ephesians 1:14 to see if you can figure out what this verse has to do with the future.

We will spend eternity praising His glory. When we see Him face to face, we will be so overwhelmed with the awesomeness of Jesus Christ that we will want to do nothing else but stand in His presence, stare at Him, and praise Him!

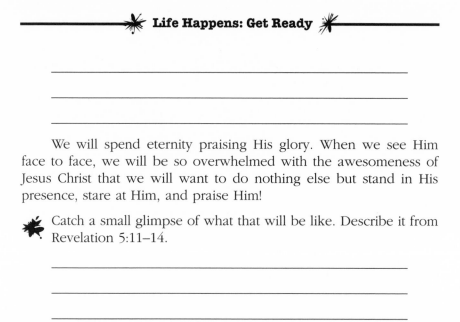 Catch a small glimpse of what that will be like. Describe it from Revelation 5:11–14.

Let this grab you and create a wild enthusiasm about your future destination—to live "to the praise of his glory."

OUR DESTINATION IS NOW

Since we will spend eternity praising His glory, it makes sense to get in plenty of practice now. Our destination now: to spend every moment of every day for the rest of our lives living "to the praise of his glory."

What does that mean? When we wake up every morning our goal is to live in a way that reflects Jesus Christ . . .

- in the way we talk
- in our attitudes
- in the way we obey and respect our parents
- in the way we treat the opposite sex
- in what we think, read, and watch.

You get the idea.

How does that work? God has given us His Holy Spirit "who is a deposit guaranteeing our inheritance" (Ephesians 1:14). Because the Holy Spirit lives in us *now* as a "deposit" we can live to the praise of his glory *now*. When we received Christ, God gave us the Holy Spirit to live in us and to change us so that we reflect Jesus Christ.

Over the years how many times have people asked us, "What are you going to be when you grow up?" Depending on our interests at the time, we answered: "A fireman." "A NBA star." "A nurse." "A lawyer."

This phrase "to the praise of his glory" changes our perspective. To begin with, we don't need to wait until we grow up or go to heaven to reach our destination. We can reach it now, today, every day. To live "to the praise of his glory" is a lifestyle, an attitude.

How did the apostle Paul express it in 2 Corinthians 3:18? (Read *The Living Bible* if possible):

_____

_____

_____

When we wake up and look in the mirror (bad hair and all), we need to become keenly aware that all day long we will be mirrors that reflect to other people who Jesus is. They will see His glory through us. They will know the attitudes, actions, and character of Jesus Christ by what they see coming out of our lives.

"Whoa!" you say. "That is heavy duty. I can't live up to that. I mess up every day. I am not perfect." So what else is new? The focus here is not on you. You are only a mirror that reflects the Holy Spirit to others. We let the Spirit of the Lord work in us. What does He do in there?

Look at what He gets rid of in Galatians 5:19–21.

_____

_____

_____

Now look at what He gives you in Galatians 5:22–23.

_____

_____

_____

He produces in us the character of Jesus Christ. We will be able to honor Christ in our . . .

> moral life,
> > thoughts,
> > > words,
> > > > relationships, and
> > > > > actions.

We are mirrors	The Holy Spirit in us provides the resources for us to "become more and more like him." The Holy Spirit takes us straight ahead to our destination to live to reflect Christ.
that reflect	We don't do that on our own. We don't need to jump higher, try harder, or do better. Instead, we have to call on God's resources to "just do it" in and through us. Over time He is
who Jesus is.	the one who will change our thoughts, our habits, our attitudes, and our actions so that we behave like Jesus Christ.

"IN 1492 COLUMBUS SAILED THE OCEAN BLUE . . ."

Because Christopher Columbus took seriously God's destination for his life, and pursued it, we have the privilege of living in America today. Even though you have never read this in a public school text, here is the real story of how he discovered America.

After his ships had been at sea much longer than antici-pated, the crew was ready to mutiny. When they con-fronted him with turning back, Columbus prayed and then requested three more days. Immediately the wind picked up and the ships moved more swiftly than at any time before. On the evening of the third day, they spotted land. He wrote in his journal later:

"It was the Lord who put it into my mind. (I could feel his hand upon me) the fact that it would be possible to sail from here to the Indies. All who heard of my project rejected it with laughter, ridi-culing me. There is no question that the inspira-tion was from the Holy Spirit, because He comforted me with rays of marvelous inspiration from the Holy Scriptures . . . . I am a most unwor-thy sinner but I have cried out to the Lord for grace and mercy, and they have covered me com-pletely. I have found the sweetest consolation since I made it my whole purpose to enjoy His marvelous presence. For the execution of the jour-ney to the Indies, I did not make use of intelli-gence, mathematics or maps. It is simply the fulfillment of [prophecy]." [1]

God's destination for us—living to reflect His glory—is the same one Christopher Columbus had. Yet each of our destinations is as uniquely significant as that of Christopher Columbus. Pursue it with a passion!

GET READY

1. Describe some of the shortcuts and wrong turns you have taken that have detained you from reaching your destination.

   _____

   _____

   _____

   _____

2. Reflecting on 2 Corinthians 3:18, look at your *future* and your *present* to determine practically three changes you need to make to live to reflect His glory. Be honest. Be specific.

   1. _____

   2. _____

   3. _____

3. Thinking about the significant way God worked out His destination for Christopher Columbus, what do you think God's significant destination is for you?

chapter 4

Look for the Billboards

How can you get where you are going and not give up on the way?

When I was a kid, every summer we headed to Florida from West Virginia for our family vacation. Just before crossing the Florida line, billboards advertised "ALL OF THE ORANGE JUICE YOU CAN DRINK FOR 10 CENTS—10 MILES." After driving another mile another sign appeared: "ALL THE ORANGE JUICE YOU CAN DRINK FOR 10 CENTS—9 MILES." Each mile another billboard appeared until, at the end of ten miles, a huge neon sign would scream, "YOU ARE HERE! ALL THE ORANGE JUICE YOU CAN DRINK FOR 10 CENTS." We always stopped at the first juice stand. As a ten-year-old I would drink ten to twelve glasses of juice. One time, after I had guzzled five or six glasses, the owner said, "Son, that's all the orange juice you can drink for ten cents."

AFTER SIGHTING THE FIRST BILLBOARD, I couldn't wait to get to the orange juice stand. I sat on the edge of my seat and read every sign we passed. God has placed some huge, neon billboards along the road to advertise what we need when we get tired, distracted, or stuck on the side of the road in pursuing our destination. Sitting on the edge of our seats, let's read every billboard and take advantage of what it offers.

SEE THE WORLD'S STRONGEST MAN (POWER)

In college I attended a Fellowship of Christian Athletes camp. One day Paul Anderson, the world's strongest man, spoke. He had won the gold medal in the Olympics and held every world weight lifting record in the world. In front of this crowd of seven or eight hundred young athletes he did several feats of strength that caused us to "ooooh" and "ahhhh." But he saved the best until last. He got ten guys from the audience to sit on a large table. Then he got under it and lifted it completely off the ground. That was more weight than anyone had lifted—ever!

"Totally impressed," described me. My mouth hung open. But that was nothing compared to the strength that God infused into Jesus Christ.

Look at the words the apostle Paul used in Ephesians 1:19–21 as he visualized how incredibly great Jesus' power is.

_____   _____

_____   _____

_____

Paul piled one power word on top of another to make the point.

"So what?" you say. "I already know that God is powerful and Jesus is strong." Yes, but Paul said this power is "for us" (Ephesians 1:19).

"But I don't feel very powerful or strong," you say. "Most of the time I feel like a spiritual wimp."

That's OK because God's power flows more freely in our weakness. According to 2 Corinthians 12:9, why do we boast in our weakness?

_____

_____

_____

When we realize how weak we are, then the power of Christ is released through us. Look at 2 Peter 1:3–4 to discover what the power of Christ gives us.

_____   _____

_____   _____

_____

When we rely totally on His power, not our own, then we have what we need to live to reflect His glory!

Now that we have the power, let's drive on down to the next billboard.

GET A FREE GIFT (GRACE)

Not one to turn down anything free, if I see a billboard advertising a free gift, I get excited.

All of us feel spiritually weak and powerless, and for good reason. According to what Paul wrote in Ephesians 2:1–3, what are those good reasons?

1. _____
2. _____
3. _____

That's worse than weak. Try dead!
Sin did that to us. Sin has left us with

- deep longings—pain in our hearts because of the disappointments of what other people have done to us.
- wrong strategies—our selfishness that tries to satisfy our deepest desires.[1]

✳ To get rid of these deep longings and wrong strategies, God has given us three free gifts. See if you can find them in Ephesians 2:5–6.

Gift 1: _____
Gift 2: _____
Gift 3: _____

Those gifts come to us as a result of His grace (vv. 5, 7–8).

We can begin to get the picture of what a big deal grace is with this definition: "God's supernatural ability in you through the cross and the resurrection."

To finish the picture, drop in these illustrations.

A Credit Card

The bank calls to tell you that they have a credit card for you that has unlimited spending which unlike our credit cards, you never have to repay. But you tell them you don't want it.

No card is like no grace. You miss out on the unlimited resources that God has made available to you in Christ. But God wants us to take it so we can cash in His grace.

A Car

On a hot summer day your car runs out of gas. Cars zoom by. You push the car until you get to a hill. Someone offers to help. And you refuse: "No, I always drive it without gas."

No gas is like no grace. We can try hard to live for God, but it is impossible. You have plenty of power under the hood, but no fuel to crank it into action. Yet when we pour in the fuel of grace, which you already have available, we will have more than enough power.

Don't get stuck on the side of the road, saying, "I can't . . . . I don't . . . . I never have . . . ." *No!* Take the gift of grace and move along to the next billboard.

LIVE IN YOUR DREAM HOUSE (RELATIONSHIPS)

> Very middle class. That describes the house I grew up in on Hale Avenue. But my parents had a dream. They bought some property that nobody wanted because it had some "undesirable elements." With almost all their savings they bought "the Hill"— about sixty acres that overlooked our town. With "sweat equity" they built a beautiful house with a fantastic view.

Imagine what your dream house would look like. How would you describe it?

_____

_____

_____

To live to reflect His glory we must move into God's dream house. How did Paul describe it in Ephesians 2:19–22?

_____

_____

_____

God has designed us to live together in unity. We should function as one brick fitting perfectly with the others. Bricks don't yell,

- "I don't like you."
- "I'm the best brick."
- "I want to be the first brick."

We could solve most problems in the church if we handled our relationships God's way.

If we have wronged someone, Jesus told us what to do (Matthew 5:23–24).

_____

_____

List anyone toward whom you have done something wrong.

_____

_____

_____

If someone has wronged us, Jesus again told us what to do (Matthew 18:15). Do you hold a grudge, feel angry, or have resentment toward another person? _____

You can't confront the other person about what he or she did to you until you release the anger you have. You can't do that honestly if you are hurt by what that person did to you. So you must get the plank out of your eye (your anger) before you try to get the speck out of your brother's eye (his hurtful action) (Matthew 7:3).

Is there anyone toward whom you have anger, resentment, or bitterness?

_____

_____

_____

Unity is God's "dream house." We help build it when we live in unity in our relationships. Then the world will look at us, like it did the early church, and say, "Gee, look how they love each other!"

Now all of us together can travel down the highway to the next billboard.

SOLVE THE MYSTERY (RELATING CHRIST)

The Great Airport Mystery, The Sinister Signpost, The House on the Cliff. I read every one of the Hardy Boys Mysteries, secretly wishing that I had their ability to find clues and courage to solve the mystery.

Now I, along with you, get to fulfill all of our mystery-solving fantasies. In fact, we are key components in solving the greatest mystery of all time.

According to Ephesians 3:6–7, what is that mystery?

_____

_____

_____

We have the incredible privilege of being detectives for the gospel. We get to find the people who have never heard the message of Christ, we search for the clue(s) that reveal the empty places in their lives, then show them how God can fill that "God-shaped vacuum" with the life-changing solution of Jesus Christ.

Most Christians feel awkward, ill-equipped, and uncomfortable as a "detective for the gospel." But it doesn't have to be that way. Practically you can do some things that will help.

- *Verbally identify with Jesus Christ.* Let people around you know that you love and follow Him.
- *Ask someone to show you how to communicate Christ.* A helpful tool is *Giving Away Your Faith.* (See page iv for ordering information).
- *Pray for three friends who need Christ.* Ask God to get them ready to receive Him.
- *Boldly tell one friend about Jesus.* Step out of your comfort zone and talk about Him. He is worth taking the relational risk.

God's desire is that we take as many people with us as possible as we pursue our destination of living to reflect His glory.

GET READY

Stop at each billboard exit and pick up the resources that will help you in living to reflect His glory.

- To release God's power I need to . . .
  (See Ephesians 1:19–21)

- To rely on God's grace I need to . . .
  (See Ephesians 2:1–6)

- To reconcile my relationships I need to . . .
  (See Ephesians 2:19–22)

- To relate Christ to unbelievers I need to . . .
  (See Ephesians 3:6–7)

chapter 5

Vote for Yourself

What is your personality, and how can you enjoy it?

Almost every high school in America has the seniors vote on senior superlatives: Best Dressed. Cutest Couple. Friendliest. Most Popular. Most Likely to Succeed. Every school has its own list. Some vote in the negative: Worst Dressed. Biggest Nerd.

One year later we see the gross inaccuracy. The Cutest Couple broke up and both go with someone else. Most Popular lives alone in the mountains. Most Likely to Succeed never made it out of summer school. The end results are understandable. After all, it's only a popularity contest.

To me the most intriguing senior superlative is Best Personality. What does that mean? Does everyone else have a mediocre personality? Does someone qualify as Worst Personality?

THE TRUTH IS THAT EVERYONE DOES have a personality, and that personality is best for him or her. That's where the problem lies. We think that if we don't have a certain personality, then we got cheated.

The first time I took a personality test, I loved it! I didn't have to take it for a grade! About halfway through, it dawned on me that everyone is unique. I remembered thinking, *What a dull world we would live in if everyone had the same kind of personality.* For the first time I realized that my personality is totally unique from everyone else's. In God's incredible creativity, He fashioned each of us into a totally unique individual, completely different from any other person.

 The psalmist expressed that uniqueness beautifully in Psalm 139:13–14. What do you think the psalm says about your unique personality?

_____

_____

_____

Because of each individual's total uniqueness, all of us can vote ourselves Best Personality. And that personality will be a major instrument God will use to move us toward His destiny for us.

Know Thyself

Socrates said it well, "Know thyself." And we need to, but not for the reasons most students pursue knowing themselves. Our culture is saturated with self-actualization, self-improvement, self-help, and self-everything else. The dominant word in the last sentence gives us a clue as to what the problem is. Understanding our personality for selfish reasons has very little value.

Jesus put the issue of knowing ourselves on a higher plane. He said, "Love the Lord your God with all your heart and . . . love your neighbor as yourself." As we discover the infinite and unique personality of God, we will learn to love Him. Out of that love relationship we will love our neighbors. With a healthy love for God and others, we will genuinely begin to love ourselves.

> **What a dull world we would live in if everyone had the same personality.**

The Heart of the Matter

The Hebrew people used the word *heart* to define personality. For example, the writer of Proverbs said, "Keep your heart with all vigilance, for from it flow the springs of life" (Proverbs 4:23, NRSV).

Out of our personality, "heart," flows life. Therefore, we need to guard our heart so it does not get messed up. Don't let anyone "stomp that sucker flat," as Lewis Grizzard would say. Put a fence around it so others don't steal it from you. Reserve it for God Himself.

The ancient Greeks divided the heart (personality) into several compartments. Note the ones in 1 Thessalonians 5:23:

1. _____

2. _____

3. _____

The "body," our physical make up—hair, ears, eyes, arms, and legs—expresses the outward, exposed dimension of our personality. The "spirit" connects to that deep inner self that has the capacity to relate to God. The spirit is what Blaise Pascal had in mind with his famous quote: "There is a God-shaped vacuum in the heart of every man that cannot be filled by any created thing, but only by God the Creator, made known through Jesus Christ." The "soul" (personality) connects the body and the spirit, the natural and the supernatural. This bridge has three unique components:

- emotions—our feelings
- mind—our thoughts
- will—our decisions

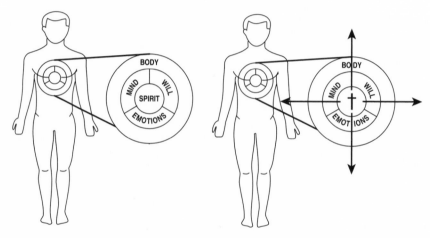

Our entire personality must be transformed because of the adverse impact of sin. That happens as we surrender our spirit to the Holy Spirit. Christ replaces self at the very heart of our personality. We are still ourselves, but Christ is in control of our spirit. Then "Christ in you" begins the process of changing our mind, will, and emotions—how we think, feel, and act. Eventually those changes are expressed through our body. At that point we are moving toward our destination, living to reflect His glory.

PERSONALITY PLUS

In 2400 B.C. Hippocrates, the famous philosopher/ physician, identified four basic personality types: "Hippocrates gave names to the temperaments that were suggested by the liquids he thought were the cause: the Sanguine—blood, Choleric—yellow bile, Melancholy—

black bile and Phlegmatic—phlegm. To him, these suggested the lively, active, black and slow temperaments."[1]

As we discover more about the four personality types, follow these ground rules.

- No one person is totally a single personality type. We are all a combination to varying degrees.
- These four personality types are broad generalizations with each one having a variety of subpatterns that reveal each person's uniqueness.
- One personality type is not better or worse than another one. Each one has strengths and weaknesses.
- We must resist the temptation to analyze, then stereotype our family and friends. Later on you can help them discover these things for themselves.
- In prayer, ask God to show you more about your personality.

THE FOCAL POINT

Positives and negatives. Strengths and weaknesses. Probably you will discover some things about your personality that you like and some you don't like. (Unless, of course, you are Choleric!) Because of our imperfections we will never have total balance in our personalities. But Jesus, the Perfect Man, was the perfect balance of all four of these personality types. Because of that, and because He lives in us to accomplish His purposes for us, He can adjust our personalities to become like His. When we release His Spirit in us, He works in our unique personality to help us live to reflect His glory. When that process is going on, we get voted Best Personality every day of the week!

GET READY

1. Take the "Discovering My Personality" survey on page 45 and then score it yourself. Follow the instructions.

To pursue this further, write or fax to Reach Out Ministries to purchase the DISC Personality Profile. The cost for each test is fifteen dollars.

Reach Out Ministries
3961 Holcomb Bridge Road
Suite 201
Norcross, GA 30092
770-441-2247
Fax: 770-449-7544

CHOLERIC (THE DOER)

Doer
Dominant
Directive
Driver
Dynamic
Determined
Developer

Motivated by:

Challenges, projects, results, and the freedom to act

Goal:

To challenge the status quo by controlling the environment and overcoming the opposition in order to achieve the desired results

Strengths and Weaknesses:

STRENGTHS	WEAKNESSES
• Overcomer	• Controversial
• Visionary	• Oblivious to risks, facts
• Decisive	• Overbearing
• Goal oriented	• Impatient
• Persistent	• Inflexible, unyielding
• Initiating	• Dictatorial
• Confident	• Braggart
• Assertive	• Blunt
• Competitive	• Abrasive
• Authoritative	• Demanding
• Independent	• Refuses help
• Results oriented	• Insensitive
• Leader	• Bossy
• Active	• Restless, workaholic
• Delegates	• Manipulative

Best Environment:
- Challenging project
- Variety in schedule and opportunities
- Freedom from control and detail

Biggest Fear:
Incompetence, being taken advantage of

Reaction to Stress:
Takes control

Suggestions for Personal Growth:

- Express empathy and emotion.
- Learn to listen.
- Relax and enjoy life.
- Be honest about weaknesses.
- Say, "I was wrong."
- Give in to others.
- Practice patience.
- Don't brag or say, "I told you so."

To determine if your personality is choleric, take the survey at the end of the chapter. If this is your personality, then intensely pursue God's vision for you. Submit your plans to Him, and pursue them with love and sensitivity. Allow yourself to be "crucified with Christ" daily so that you go after goals that are God's goals and not your own. Then God will help you overcome your weaknesses and will use you to impact the world for Christ.[2]

SANGUINE (THE INFLUENCER)

Influencer
Initiator
Inspirer
Interest in people
Interacter

Motivated by:

People, approval, and recognition

Goal:

To persuade others by creating an environment that motivates and assembles people to influence others

Strengths and Weaknesses:

STRENGTHS	WEAKNESSES
• Optimistic	• Overselling
• Enthusiastic	• Manipulative
• Personable	• Self-centered
• Charismatic	• Emotional
• Confident	• Overconfident
• Communicative	• Compulsive talker
• Persuasive	• Poor listener
• Gregarious	• Superficial
• Sense of humor	• Exaggerative
• Compassionate	• Angers easily
• Life of the party	• Disorganized
• Memory for stories	• Bored with detail
• Innocent	• Naive
• Good on stage	• Insecure

Best Environment:
- Freedom from control and detail
- Opportunity to influence others
- Friendly

Biggest Fear:
Rejection

Reaction to Stress:
Attacks verbally

Suggestions for Personal Growth:
- Listen more.
- Discipline yourself to follow through.
- Control your time and emotions.
- Condense your conversation.
- Follow through on friendships.
- Say no to extra responsibilities.
- Be sensitive to others.
- Don't come on so strong.

To discover if you are a sanguine personality, take the survey at the end of the chapter. If this is your primary personality type, then rejoice that God will use you to have such a persuasive influence on people, and make it a goal to increase your effectiveness by asking God to help you discipline yourself to overcome your weaknesses.

PHLEGMATIC (THE RELATER)

Sympathetic
Stable
Steady
Sensitive
Security conscious
Supportive

Motivated by:
Relationships and appreciation

Goal:
To support the present environment by encouraging positive relationships and specializing in specific tasks and consistent roles

Strengths and Weaknesses:

STRENGTHS	WEAKNESSES
• Loyal	• Avoids conflict
• Supportive	• Unenthusiastic
• Agreeable	• Conforming
• Relational	• Possessive
• Easy-going, relaxed	• Complacent
• Balanced	• Indecisive
• Consistent	• Limited goals
• Sympathetic and kind	• Fearful and worried
• Diplomatic	• Unspoken expectations
• Dependable	• Undisciplined
• Reluctant leader	• Misses opportunities
• Sincere	• Lenient
• Quiet listener	• Spectator
• Contented	• Lethargic

Best Environment:
- Specialized opportunities with parameters
- Working with a team consistently
- Supportive appreciation

Biggest Fear:
Loss of security

Reaction to Stress:
Passively yields

Suggestions for Personal Growth:
- Acknowledge self-worth.
- Take initiative to participate.
- Set goals.
- Don't procrastinate.
- Make key decisions daily.
- Broaden range of friendships.

To discover if you have a phlegmatic personality, take the survey at the end of the chapter. If this is your primary personality type, discover how God can use you to build positive, long-term relationships that will support your present environment. Ask God to help you take initiative to overcome your weaknesses.

MELANCHOLY (THE THINKER)

Contemplator
Conscientious
Competent
Creative
Controlled
Correct/analytical
Calculating
Compliant

Motivated by:

Excellence, accuracy, protection, and security

Goal:

To accurately create a product that meets the highest standards of excellence

Strengths and Weaknesses:

STRENGTHS	WEAKNESSES
• Precise	• Too careful
• Orderly	• Picky
• Thorough	• Too detailed
• Cautious	• Too cautious
• Analytical	• Analysis paralysis
• Systematic	• Obsessive/compulsive
• Accurate	• Indecisive
• Conscientious	• Detached
• Adaptable	• Sensitive
• Creative	• Finicky
• Quiet	• Withdrawn
• Self-sacrificing	• Martyr complex
• Faithful	• Too involved
• Perfectionist	• Judgmental
• Thinker	• Depressed
• Humble	• Self-negating

Best Environment:
- Supportive and predictable
- Clearly defined standards of excellence
- Operating with precision and accuracy

Biggest Fear:
Criticism, change

Reaction to Stress:
Withdraws

Suggestions for Personal Growth:
- Loosen the grip on perfection.
- Don't take it personally.
- Risk verbalizing your feelings.
- Think positively.
- Control emotional highs and lows.
- Respect others with their imperfections.
- Accept change.

Take the survey at the end of the chapter to find out if you have a melancholy personality. If this is your primary personality type, then analyze how God will use you to create artistry and excellence in the body of Christ. Design a plan to increase your effectiveness, and ask God to help you overcome your weaknesses.

DISCOVERING MY PERSONALITY TEST

Each of us is a combination of the four basic personality types. No one particular personality is any better or any worse than the others. They are all different. Therefore, there are no right or wrong answers.

In each of the twenty-four lines on the next page, you have a choice of four words or phrases. Choose the word or phrase that best describes you when you are with your family and your friends.

Follow these two steps to complete the test.

1. Circle the one word or phrase on each of the twenty-four lines that best describes you. Circle only one per line. Choose the word or phrase that describes how you really are, not what others expect of you, or how you wish you were.

2. Determine your score by locating the word or phrase on line 1 that you circled and matching it to the column letter at the top. Find line 1 of the Scoring Sheet and locate the matching letter. Circle the column letter. It will not necessarily be the same column as the test.

For example, on line 1 if you circled "daring, pioneering," it is under column B. Go to line 1 on the Scoring Sheet and circle the "B." You will note that it is now under column 1.

Once you have transferred all answers from the test to the Scoring Sheet, add up the total number of circles in each column and place that number on the line at the bottom of that column. These four numbers should total twenty-four.

The column you score highest in is your dominant personality type.

Column 1—Choleric (The Doer)
Column 2—Sanguine (The Influencer)
Column 3—Phlegmatic (The Relater)
Column 4—Melancholy (The Thinker)

Now that you know your personality type review the characteristics of your personality on pages 37–44.[3]

DISCOVERING YOUR PERSONALITY SURVEY

Directions: Circle ONE phrase in each row that you feel describes you best.

	A	B	C	D
1.	gentle, kind	daring, pioneering	humble, mild-mannered	persuasive
2.	stubborn	careful	likable	considerate
3.	patient	sociable	bold	analytical
4.	decisive	listens	easy going	free-spirited
5.	precise, accurate	funny	slow to get angry	forceful
6.	inspiring	self-reliant	tactful with words	thinks of others
7.	perfectionist	team-player	will not give up	wants to have fun
8.	motivator	brave	unsure	mediator
9.	friendly	exact	even-tempered	competitive
10.	thinks things through	shows feelings	insistent	balanced
11.	decision-maker	sacrificing	mild-mannered	talkative
12.	easily pleased	respectful	full of life	daring
13.	enthusiastic	aggressive	tends to worry	easy going
14.	cautious	understanding	takes charge	gets agreement
15.	expresses emotion	detailed	agreeable	loves challenges
16.	confident	animated	one thing at a time	analytical
17.	self-disciplined	suspicious	lively	predictable
18.	energetic	kind	adventurous	chooses carefully
19.	quiet	positive	willing to please	tries new things
20.	argumentative	examines closely	easily led	does not worry
21.	demanding	trusting	contented	critical of self
22.	repetitious	indecisive	has many friends	controlling
23.	supportive, helpful	fun to be with	decides carefully	outspoken
24.	gets along easily	questioning	popular	wants change

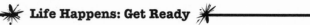

SCORING SHEET

1.	B	D	A	C
2.	A	C	D	B
3.	C	B	A	D
4.	A	D	C	B
5.	D	B	C	A
6.	B	A	D	C
7.	C	D	B	A
8.	B	A	D	C
9.	D	A	C	B
10.	C	B	D	A
11.	A	D	C	B
12.	D	C	A	B
13.	B	A	D	C
14.	C	D	B	A
15.	D	A	C	B
16.	A	B	C	D
17.	B	C	D	A
18.	C	A	B	D
19.	D	B	C	A
20.	A	D	C	B
21.	A	B	C	D
22.	D	C	B	A
23.	D	B	A	C
24.	D	C	A	B

_____   _____   _____   _____

My personality type is _____.

6

Pull Out the Credit Card

What are your spiritual gifts, and how can you use them?

"Hey, Dad, can I have some money?"

Have you ever said that before? What was your dad's response?

- "No!"
- "Not in your lifetime."
- "Not again."
- "Do you think money grows on trees?"
- "This is it! That's all! No more!"

Why does he give a negative response? Money doesn't grow on trees. Resources are limited.

It would blow you away if sometime he said, "Sure, how much do you need? Spend all you want. Here's my credit card. Have a great time!"

GOD HAS ISSUED US A CREDIT CARD with unlimited resources. We can use the card whenever we need it. Through what He gives us we have enough for other people too. And unlike our credit cards, we never have to pay it off. Here's how it works.

> God's grace in us
>   gives spiritual gifts to us
>   to accomplish God's work through us.

Some people are afraid of spiritual gifts. They think, "I'm not getting into this because once you discuss spiritual gifts, then handling snakes can't be far behind." Yet without spiritual gifts we lack power to overcome the forces of darkness. With them we bring the power of Christ into any situation. Spiritual gifts are vital to discovering our destiny, according to Romans 12:6. Check it out.

GOD'S GRACE IN US

Charis

We came into a relationship with Christ by the grace of God (Ephesians 2:8–9). At that point we received The Gift—Jesus Christ Himself. The Greek word for grace is *charis*. Grace is . . .

God's
Riches
At
Christ's
Expense

Charisma

When we entered into a relationship with Jesus, He placed His Holy Spirit within us. The Greek word for that is *charisma*. We have the gift of the Holy Spirit continually pouring into us and filling us up, like a spring bubbling inside us, giving us the resources we need to live the Christian life.

Charismata

Part of what we receive are spiritual gifts. The Greek word for gifts is *charismata* ("gracelets"), little graces or spiritual gifts. All of our little gifts come from the big gift of grace.

Char

When we use those gifts, they bring great joy. The Greek word for joy is *char*. Not only do we experience joy ourselves when we use our gifts, but also we bring joy to others.

GOD GIVES SPIRITUAL GIFTS TO US

Since spiritual gifts come from the Holy Spirit, certainly we do not want to misuse them any more than we would want to misuse a valuable credit card. Avoid these errors:

1. "My spiritual gifts are my natural talents and abilities." A beautiful singing voice is not a spiritual gift; it is a natural talent. We don't measure our effectiveness for Christ by our talents and abilities. What we have to offer God *naturally* isn't enough. Spiritual gifts allow us *supernaturally* to tap into the resources of God.

2. "Spiritual gifts are not for today." The overwhelming needs of people today require us to conclude that only by releasing God's power through spiritual gifts can we make a difference in people's lives.

3. "Only mature Christians can use spiritual gifts." The Bible never equates spiritual maturity with spiritual gifts.

4. "I will choose my spiritual gift." We don't choose our spiritual gifts. God chooses them and then gives them to us. The emphasis is not on us, but on Him.

Avoiding these errors frees us to use our spiritual gifts more wisely.

On the positive side we will use our gifts better when we understand who they are for. The credit card has your name on it.

- Every Christian has spiritual gifts. When you received Christ, He brought with Him the gifts of the Spirit. How did the apostle express that in 1 Peter 4:10?

_____

_____

_____

- Each one of us has received the very best gifts for us. God wants us to have the very best gifts possible so He picked them out personally and then delivered them individually to us. How did the apostle Paul make that point in 1 Corinthians 12:11?

_____

_____

_____

To Accomplish His Work through Us

Like strong muscles give strength to our physical bodies, spiritual gifts put to use make the body of Christ strong. Spiritual gifts are the "muscle" to the body of Christ. When I broke my wrist and had my arm in a cast for six weeks, I learned how quickly muscles atrophy when they are not in use. Conversely, lifting weights three times a week builds my muscles. That is why the apostle Paul challenged the Romans regarding spiritual gifts, "let him use it" (Romans 12:6).

Check out what happens to the body of Christ when we use our gifts.

- 1 Corinthians 14:26

_____

_____

_____

- 1 Corinthians 12:12, 22

_____

_____

_____

- 1 Corinthians 12:25–26

_____

_____

_____

The apostle Paul split the different spiritual gifts into three categories in 1 Corinthians 12:4–6.

1. "different kinds of gifts"—grace gifts
2. "different kinds of service"—service gifts
3. "different kinds of working"—working gifts*

Each of these three groups of gifts serves a different purpose. Let's take a closer look so we can know the gifts God has for us and how to use them to pursue our destiny.

GRACE GIFTS

These gifts come directly from God's grace and give us *motivation* for ministry. They give us the energy to build God's kingdom. We find these gifts in Romans 12:6–8.

---

* All gifts are an extension of God's grace. Yet here and in the other passages about gifts the apostle Paul places the gifts in different categories. In 1 Corinthians 12:4–6 he uses three words for gifts: (1) *Charismaton,* which means "grace." In Romans 12:6 he uses the same word for gifts, referring to spiritual gifts of grace. He gives a list of those gifts. (2) *Diakonian,* which means "service." In Ephesians 4:12 he uses the same word after listing the gifts. (3) *Energematon,* which means "work" and from which we get the word *energy.* This word indicates power that is in operation. This energy or power manifests itself in spiritual gifts. Paul then gives a list of the gifts that manifest themselves in 1 Corinthians 12:7–11. This is a helpful way of looking at the gifts but by no means the only way of approaching it.

1. Prophesying. A prophet brings messages from God to people, usually revealing ungodly motives and attitudes in others.
2. Serving. A servant demonstrates love by meeting practical needs.
3. Teaching. A teacher researches and validates truth, then helps others understand this truth.
4. Encouraging. An encourager stimulates the faith of others.
5. Giving. A giver entrusts resources to others to carry out the ministry.
6. Leading. A leader coordinates the activities of others to achieve common goals.
7. Showing mercy. A merciful person identifies with and comforts those in distress.

> While you are eating lunch at a fast-food restaurant someone slips. The tray of burgers, fries, and drinks flies through the air and crashes to the floor. Food covers a ten-foot radius. All around people stare and snicker.

How would you respond as a

1. *Prophet?* "That's what happens when you're not careful."
2. *Servant?* "Let me help you clean it up."
3. *Teacher?* "You fell because the floor was slick and the tray was too heavy on one side."
4. *Encourager?* "Next time walk more slowly and carry your tray with both hands. It won't happen again."
5. *Giver?* "I'll buy you another lunch."
6. *Leader?* "Tom, let's clean up. You get the mop, and Sue, you get the tray."
7. *Merciful person?* "Don't feel too bad. It could happen to the best of us."

Your response to this situation will give you an idea of what your "grace gift" might be.

SERVICE GIFTS

These *ministries* give us opportunities to take action and serve others (1 Pet. 4:10). They fit against a backdrop of love that cares deeply about other people. Before the apostle Peter launched into an explanation of service gifts, he said, "Above all, love each other deeply, because love covers over a multitude of sins" (1 Pet. 4:8). Because we love, we serve with our gifts, giving them freely to minister to others.

Let's summarize these gifts as found in Ephesians 4:11; 1 Peter 4:10, and 1 Corinthians 12:27–31.

1. Apostles. Apostles are those sent forth with authority to advance the kingdom of God and build up the church.
2. Prophets. Prophets speak for God.
3. Evangelists. Evangelists announce the good news of Jesus publicly and privately and equip Christians to witness to their faith.
4. Pastors. Pastors shepherd the flock with care and guidance.
5. Teachers. Teachers search the Word of God and explain it to others.
6. Miracle workers. Miracle workers do signs and wonders to build up the church and to demonstrate the power of God to an unbelieving world.
7. Healers. Healers bring physical, emotional, and spiritual healing to people.
8. Helpers. Helpers serve by meeting needs, particularly those of the poor and sick.
9. Administrators. Administrators give leadership to the church.
10. Tongues-speakers. Those who speak in tongues communicate with God in a special prayer language.

The grace/motivation gifts are put into practice in the context of these service/ministry gifts. Once you discover your grace gift, you find a place to put it into practice through one of the service gifts.

WORKING GIFTS

This set of gifts offers *manifestations* or outward expressions as a result of the Holy Spirit working in our lives. In 1 Corinthians 12:7–11, the word *manifestation* means God gives to us these different gifts, giving one here and one there at various times and in various situations. As opposed to grace gifts, which we have permanently, these gifts come and go. We never *possess* them, we *express* them. Why? God wants to give us just what we need to meet the situation of the moment.

1. Wisdom. Wisdom is seeing from God's point of view.
2. Knowledge. Knowledge is gaining insight into a specific situation.
3. Faith. Faith is visualizing what God wants to do.
4. Healing. Healing means giving spiritual, emotional, or physical health.

5. Miraculous powers. Miraculous powers means allowing God to demonstrate His power supernaturally.

6. Prophecy. Prophecy is expressing the message of God to others.

7. Discernment. Discernment is perceiving hidden attitudes.

8. Tongues. Tongues means communicating with God in a special prayer language.

9. Interpretation of tongues. Interpretation of tongues means translating spiritual truth after someone speaks in tongues.

These gifts are given "for the common good." When these gifts operate, then everyone in the body profits as a result.

From each person's *grace gift* (motivation) can come a variety of different *service gifts* (ministry). When someone exercises his or her service gift, then any number of *working gifts* (manifestations) can be expressed.

Discovering Your Spiritual Gifts

At this point you must be asking, "So how do I discover my spiritual gifts?" Follow these practical steps.

1. *Believe.* Trust that God has given you spiritual gifts. Jesus lives in you, and God has promised His gifts to you. Open your heart and mind to what the Lord has for you. Don't reject your gifts because of your past experience, fear, lack of knowledge, or preconceived ideas. To gain the appropriate attitude about this, respond to Romans 12:3.

   _____

   _____

   _____

2. *Receive.* If Christ lives in you, you already have spiritual gifts. Ask God to show you what they are. Let James 4:2 encourage you.

   _____

   _____

   _____

   Pray a prayer like this: "Lord Jesus, Giver of all good and perfect gifts, I desire to receive the gifts You have for me. Would You show me what they are and how to use them?"

3. *Study.* Make a thorough study of spiritual gifts. Reread: Romans 12:3–8; Ephesians 4:11–13; 1 Corinthians 12:27–31; 1 Peter 4:10; 1 Corinthians 12:7–11; and 1 Corinthians 14.

4. *Confirm.* Your desires and experiences and the advice of others all fit into the discovery process. Use these practical hints to confirm your gifts.

   - Take the spiritual gifts test. What did it say about your gifts?
   - Examine your personal desires. What do you enjoy doing most? This gives you a clue to what your gifts are, but it is not necessarily conclusive.
   - Experiment with your gifts. If you are not sure what your gifts are, then try the ones you think might be yours. When you try one, if it is yours, then you will enjoy the challenge of using it.
   - Talk to people you respect. Go over this material with your pastor, youth minister, or respected friend. Get their input.

5. *Respond.* With gifts come opportunities to use them. As you do, you will discover and confirm your gifts. How does God want you to use your gifts to minister to others?

   - Use your gifts to energize the body of Christ. The Great Commandment is to love God with all of our hearts, and to love our neighbors as ourselves (Matthew 22:36–38). By using our gifts we energize others with love and build up the body of Christ.
   - Use your gifts to evangelize the lost. The Great Commission tells us to "go and make disciples of all nations" (Matthew 28:18–20). When we exercise our spiritual gifts around non-Christians, then God will use us to bring people to Christ.[1]

GET READY

1. Take the Spiritual Gifts Survey at the end of the chapter, and then talk to others about what you discover.

2. Determine the best place for you to experiment with your spiritual gifts this week. Try using your motivation gift and record how that worked out.

SPIRITUAL GIFTS SURVEY

Introduction

This survey[2] is designed to help you discover your basic motivational gift. It is not a foolproof method; however, it will provide a guideline. For some who take the survey, it will become obvious what their spiritual gift is. For others it will help them to narrow down to two or three the most likely possibilities.

Instructions in Taking the Survey

1. Please answer every question. Do not leave any questions blank.

2. There are no right or wrong answers to any of the questions. Answer the questions as they apply to you.

3. Mark the answers with

+ (usually characterizes me)
o (sometimes characterizes me)
– (hardly ever characterizes me)

Scoring Instructions

1. Complete the survey, answering every question.

2. On the page entitled "Tally Sheet for Spiritual Gift Survey," add the numbers for each category to discover the total. The one you have the most of is your primary motivation gift.

IDENTIFYING YOUR SPIRITUAL GIFTS

1. I easily recall specific likes and dislikes of people.
2. I enjoy making wise purchases and investments.
3. When another person has problems, I like to see what needs to be done and offer steps of action.
4. I am free to feel happy or sad when I am with an individual or group.
5. I like to discover and meet practical needs, especially manual projects.
6. I have a desire to give money to valuable projects or ministries.
7. I avoid giving people information that lacks practical application to their lives.

8. I am attracted to and understand people who are in distress.
9. I have the desire to meet needs as quickly as possible.
10. I give my money hoping to get others to give.
11. I have the ability to see how people's problems can help them reach new levels of maturity.
12. I have a desire to remove hurts and bring healing to others.
13. I don't get tired when I meet others' needs.
14. I see financial needs that others might overlook.
15. I have more concern for people's mental distress than for their physical distress.
16. I am willing to use my personal funds to avoid delaying a project.
17. I enjoy meeting needs without someone putting pressure on me to do it.
18. I like to discover insights from people's human experiences that can be backed up in Scripture.
19. I avoid confrontation unless I see how it will benefit another person.
20. I like to see a job completed, even if I have to give extra effort to finish it.
21. I enjoy it when my money is an answer to specific prayer.
22. I like it when people are eager to follow potential steps of action.
23. I am sensitive to words and actions that hurt other people.
24. I consult with another person to confirm the amount of a gift I want to give.
25. I don't like it when someone teaches me something that does not have practical steps of action.
26. I have the ability to sense sincere motives in other people.
27. I am involved in a variety of activities and find it difficult to say no.
28. I have a concern that my money goes to quality individuals and ministries.
29. I enjoy talking to people when it results in new insights for them.
30. I enjoy short-range goals but get frustrated with long-range goals.
31. I like to feel a part of the people or work to whom I give my money.
32. I feel close to those who are sensitive to the needs and feelings of others.
33. I experience frustration when time limits are attached to jobs.
34. I do not feel close to those who are insincere or insensitive.
35. I like to verbally express what God has shown me.

36. I have the ability to see the big picture and to set long-range goals.
37. I believe that the gift of teaching is the foundation for all other gifts.
38. I can discern the character and motives of others.
39. I like to organize the things for which I am responsible.
40. I like words to be accurate when I talk and write.
41. I am able to identify, define, and hate evil.
42. I like to complete tasks as quickly as possible.
43. I like to challenge the knowledge of those who teach me.
44. I am willing to confess my sins if it encourages others to confess theirs.
45. I like to know the resources available to me to complete a task.
46. I like to do research in order to prove the truth of the Bible.
47. I like to depend on the Bible as my highest authority.
48. I know what can or cannot be delegated.
49. I like to see people's behavior change to match their convictions.
50. I like to move on to a new challenge.
51. I like to systematically study and teach the Bible.
52. I like to speak to others directly to persuade them to action.
53. I tend to assume leadership if no structured leader exists.
54. I don't like illustrations unless they come from the Bible.
55. I have a deep concern for God's reputation.
56. I will endure negative reactions from workers in order to accomplish the task.
57. I get turned off by illustrations from the Bible that are out of context.
58. I hurt over the sins of others.
59. I get excited when a plan comes together, and I enjoy seeing the finished product.
60. I enjoy doing detailed research of the Bible more than I enjoy presenting it.
61. I like to help other people see their personal weaknesses.
62. I like people to pay attention when I speak to them.
63. I like to test myself against principles in the Bible.

TALLY SHEET FOR SPIRITUAL GIFT SURVEY

Instructions: Add the numbers under each category.

2 points for +
1 point for o
0 points for –

Serving

1 ____   5 ____   9 ____   13 ____   16 ____   20 ____   27 ____   30 ____   33 ____

Total _____

Giving

2 ____   6 ____   10 ____   14 ____   17 ____   21 ____   24 ____   28 ____   31 ____

Total _____

Exhortation

3 ____   7 ____   11 ____   18 ____   22 ____   25 ____   29 ____   35 ____   62 ____

Total _____

Mercy

4 ____   8 ____   12 ____   15 ____   19 ____   23 ____   26 ____   32 ____   34 ____

Total _____

Prophecy

38 ____   41 ____   44 ____   47 ____   49 ____   52 ____   55 ____   58 ____   61 ____

Total _____

Leadership

36 ____   39 ____   42 ____   45 ____   48 ____   50 ____   53 ____   56 ____   59 ____

Total _____

Teaching

37 ____   40 ____   43 ____   46 ____   51 ____   54 ____   57 ____   60 ____   63 ____

Total _____

chapter 7

Go for the Best

What are your abilities and experiences, and how can you maximize them?

Comic books! I love 'em! When I was growing up, I read all kinds. I collected them. All of the comics had one thing in common. The back page had the Charles Atlas ad. Always the same, the headline read: "ARE YOU TIRED OF BEING A 6 FOOT, 90 POUND WEAKLING?" "Yep," I said. I read on. The first frame was a skinny guy and a beautiful girl at the beach together. In the second frame a muscular bully kicked sand in the skinny guy's face. In the third frame "Mr. Muscle" strolled off with the girl. The fourth frame showed the skinny guy kicking a chair and yelling, "I'm tired of being a 6 foot, 90 pound weakling!" He filled out the Charles Atlas coupon in the fifth frame. In the sixth frame he received his Charles Atlas kit and began working out. Six weeks later, in the seventh frame, our frail friend had transformed into Mr. Olympia. In the final frame he got the girl back.

Every comic book I opened, I read the Charles Atlas ad. Why? I identified with the skinny kid. I hoped my body would change. It never happened!

EVERYTHING AROUND US "SUCKERS" us into the world's view of what we are supposed to look like, smell like, and dress like, but God does not look at our potential the way the world does.

WAY BEYOND US

Do you ever dream about your future? your potential? Certainly! But rarely do we dream big enough. Usually we dream in light of our limited abilities and confined experiences. God wants to work through our abilities and experiences to move beyond them.

When Jesus asked the disciples, "Who do you say I am?" Peter, the disciple, responded with limited potential written all over him. When we look at Peter's abilities and experiences, we wonder how the Lord could ever use him.

- He had "foot in mouth disease." At the holy moment of the transfiguration with Jesus in deep conversation with Moses and Elijah, Peter broke the mood with his inappropriate comment. What was it? Read Matthew 17:4.

_____

_____

_____

- He appeared to have an IQ just above plant life. (Well, not quite that bad!) For three years Jesus had talked of peace and love. When the soldiers came to arrest Jesus, Peter forgot it all. He pulled his sword. What did he do then? Read Matthew 26:51.

_____

_____

_____

- He was rude and crude. When Jesus made it clear to His disciples that He had to go to Jerusalem to die, Peter had a few choice words for Him. What did he say? Read Matthew 16:22.

_____

_____

- He exhibited little self-discipline. Jesus had told Peter, along with the other disciples, to watch and pray. What did they do instead? Read Matthew 26:39–44.

_____

_____

_____

- He was filled with fear. Peter protested that if everyone else abandoned Jesus he would not. How did he fulfill that vow? Read Matthew 26:69–75.

_____

_____

_____

- In spite of Peter's inabilities and lack of experience, he answered Jesus' question "Who do you say I am?" correctly. In one of the greatest statements ever uttered, what did he proclaim? Read Matthew 16:16.

_____

_____

_____

God took the limited abilities and experiences of this common fisherman, converted them, and then used Peter to glorify Him. He established His church on Peter, the rock. God wants to take our limited abilities and experiences, convert them, and then use us to do things that are way beyond us. He wants us to live to reflect His glory.

CONVERTED TO THE CAUSE

Where Peter may have had limited talents, the apostle Paul was totally different. He had terrific talent.

- He had business skills. As a rabbi, according to Jewish practice, Paul had to have a trade. He could take no money for preaching, so he made his living by his own work. According to Acts 18:2, what did Paul do for a living?

_____

_____

- He was a genius. He had mega-intelligence. Look at Acts 18:4 and 22:3 to see how we know that.

_____

_____

_____

- He was sophisticated. We know that Paul possessed Roman citizenship, indicating that he was a man of culture (Acts 22:28).
  But he had a dark side. Zealous in all he did, Paul had it out for the young church. From Acts 7:59–8:3, what two specific acts of terror did he commit?

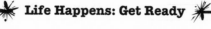

1. _____

_____

2. _____

_____

All of these positive abilities and negative experiences God tapped when He met this man on the Damascus Road and converted his skill, intelligence, culture, and misplaced zeal toward one cause—taking the gospel to the Gentiles. The apostle Paul lived to reflect His glory.

As He did with Peter and Paul, God wants to convert our abilities and experiences and use them for His cause.

What is the principle here? People have talent—some less, some more. People have experiences that are part of their lives—some bad, some good. In it all God converts our abilities and experiences, and then uses them to accomplish His purpose.

With that in mind, how can we maximize our abilities and experiences for God's purpose?

1. *Understand that everyone has unique abilities and experiences.* One of the most common excuses people give for not getting involved is, "I just don't have anything to offer."

That seems to be what one person thought in Luke 19:11–27. How do you think the one-talent guy felt? Why do you think he responded the way he did?

_____

_____

_____

Each of those servants had some significant things going for them. They had

- something to invest
- the responsibility to invest it
- time to make the investment
- the promise of a return on the investment
- the promise of multiplied rewards for making the investment

What was true of those servants is true for us. But like the servant who didn't invest his talent, often we fall prey to common myths about what God has given us to invest.

- Myth 1: I have very few skills.
- Myth 2: I can't do much because I was not born with skills.
- Myth 3: Valuable skills are learned primarily in the classroom.
- Myth 4: If I have skills, I will know I have them.
- Myth 5: Skills I use at work or school cannot be used elsewhere.

The truth is that each of us have certain talents. National studies show that the average person possesses five hundred to seven hundred skills. Some may be sharpened in the classroom, others by experience. Through experience we begin to identify our many skills. We may use them in our work, but we also can use them in ministry. Our unique abilities and experiences open the way for God to use us uniquely.

2. *Quit comparing ourselves to others.* When we crank up the comparison approach, we get our nose bloodied badly.

THE WORLD SAYS	WE SAY
"Look glamorous."	"I look average."
"Be wealthy."	"I'm struggling to pay for my sneakers."
"Act macho."	"I'm a wimp."
"Be intelligent."	"I feel dumb."
"Athletes are cool."	"I'm spastic."
"Rock stars are heroes."	"I can hardly play the radio."

In the spiritual realm it's even worse. We know we should read the Bible, pray, and witness. When we go to church and hang around Bobby Bible Study, Priscilla Prayer, and Wally Witness, we get intimidated quickly.

If we accept the world's view of success, then we will always feel inferior. We will never measure up.

However, the apostle Paul lifted us out of that pit with a fresh perspective in 2 Corinthians 10:12. How is his perspective different than what we usually hear?

_____

_____

_____

Practically, we can quit comparing ourselves to others by agreeing with God daily:

- God created my unique self.
- He put me together in my mother's womb.
- His works are wonderful.
- When He made me, He did not make a mistake. He made me so unique that, like the snowflake, there is no one else like me (Psalm 139:13–14).

At a prestigious southern college I learned this lesson. I decided to major in history. I made a 74 on my first history test. Redoubling my effort, I made a 47 on the second test. So much for history! My roommate became a Fulbright scholar. A fraternity brother earned a Rhodes scholarship. By comparison I felt dumb and dumber. I didn't measure up. In a vicious cycle I beat up on myself by comparing myself to these very intelligent people. But then I made the revolutionary discovery that I have "the mind of Christ" (1 Corinthians 2:16). In time I quit comparing myself to other people, and God began to use my unique mind to communicate His thoughts to others.

3. *Maximize strengths and minimize weaknesses.* Write your name in the box.

Now write your name with your opposite hand.

Quite a difference! When we can't write with our preferred hand, it makes us feel uncomfortable. Writing takes extra time and effort, and we do a lousy job of it. But when we write with the hand that has "ability and experience," we not only feel comfortable at it, but also we do it quickly and excellently. We never think, *I need to work on writing with my other hand.* Why? We build on our strength, not fret over our weakness.[1]

When I ask people, "What are your five greatest strengths?" they struggle to answer me. When I say, "Tell me your five greatest weaknesses," they do it in a heartbeat. We tend to focus more on our weaknesses than on our strengths. How can we turn that around and build on our strengths?

- Realize that God did not design us to do everything. A friend once said to me, "Barry, you're the kind of person who likes to eat the whole pizza in one bite." He observed correctly that I want to do it all. From him I learned to focus only on doing the few things God has given me to do.
- Recognize that we will never have some abilities, no matter how hard we try. I could practice sixteen hours a day and never become an accomplished musician. I just don't have it. The psalmist gave us God's perspective: "I praise you because I am fearfully and wonderfully made; your works are wonderful" (Psalm 139:14). God made us "wonderfully," even without some abilities because He can use us best that way.
- Turn difficult experiences into opportunities. Victimized by our background or scarred by sinful choices, difficult experiences have created in us weaknesses that have to be overcome. Simon Peter had those weaknesses too. He swore allegiance to Jesus loudly and then denied Jesus because of his fatal flaw of wanting to please everyone. But the Holy Spirit turned that flaw—his fear of rejection—into fearlessness. Peter boldly led three thousand people to Christ in one day.

  As president of the student body in high school, I gave a speech in assembly every week. Fearful and insecure, I wrote the speeches out word for word and read them. Once Jesus took hold in me, He turned my fear of speaking into something I enjoy so much I do it for a living.

Grapple with these ideas and apply them to your situation by asking God what He had in mind in 2 Corinthians 12:9.

_____

_____

_____

- Concentrate on inward strength, not outward ability. In our society, ability, beauty, and talent are gods. But the true God cares more about character than coolness. When God sent Samuel to find a king for Israel, immediately Samuel saw Jesse's handsome son, Eliab, and thought he had found the king. Samuel then learned that God had a better idea. What was it and why? Read 1 Samuel 16:7.

_____

_____

_____

_____

Carol and I have tried to capture that with our kids, since they were very young. I wish I had a dollar for every time I have told my girls, "To be pretty on the outside, you have to be pretty on the inside." Character comes when we learn to obey Christ.

- Cooperate with God to finish the job. God is not finished with us yet. He will continue to sharpen our strengths and minimize our weaknesses. According to Romans 8:28–29, what are the results?

_____

_____

_____

_____

4. _Give our best to serve others for God's glory._ How do you think God views our abilities and experiences?

If we are

- athletically gifted, does He want us to be a star?
- physically attractive, does He want us to become a model, actress, or homecoming queen?
- musically talented, does He want us to sing publicly?
- intelligent, does He want us to make all A's or big bucks?

Many people lose touch with God's plan right here. In fact, many become bitter because they asked God to make them a success, and in their view He didn't do it. Why not? God is not into producing superstars, but servants. He operates on a higher principle than our personal success. Discover His rule of thumb in 1 Corinthians 10:31.

_____

_____

_____

The bottom line: God wants us to use our abilities and experiences to serve others for His glory.

When we put God ahead of our own success, then we free ourselves to excel in every area of life for the glory of God. Jesus modeled that when He washed His disciples' feet. Then He said, "Now that I, your Lord and Teacher, have washed your feet, you also should wash one another's feet" (John 13:14). Jesus had the ability and experience to do anything, but He chose to serve others for God's glory. He challenges us to do the same. When we do, serving becomes the gateway to our destiny!

GET READY

1. Take the Abilities Survey on this page.
2. Take the Experiences Survey on page 69.
3. Ask your parents if they agree with your conclusions.

ABILITIES SURVEY

Make a list of your five most fulfilling accomplishments.

1. _____

2. _____

3. _____

4. _____

5. _____

Now go back and circle the verbs that show the actions you performed in each achievement.

Now check the five most significant abilities you have.

- Entertain: perform, act, dance, speak, model, sing
- Recruit: enlist, motivate people to get involved
- Interview: discover what others are really like
- Research: read, gather information, collect data
- Draw: conceptualize, picture, paint, photograph, cartoon, caricature
- Graph: lay out, design, create visual displays or banners
- Evaluate: analyze data and draw conclusions
- Plan: strategize, design, and organize programs and events
- Manage: supervise people and coordinate the details to accomplish a task
- Counsel: listen, encourage, guide with sensitivity
- Teach: explain, demonstrate, tutor, train
- Write: produce articles, letters, books
- Edit: rewrite, proofread
- Promote: advertise events and activities
- Repair: fix, restore, maintain
- Feed: create meals for large or small groups
- Recall: remember names, faces, or information
- Mechanically operate: use equipment, tools, or machinery
- Resource: search out inexpensive approaches
- Account: work with numbers, data, or money
- Classify: systematize and file books, data, records, material
- Relate: deal with people with care and courtesy
- Welcome: develop rapport, convey warmth, make people feel comfortable
- Compose: write music, lyrics
- Landscape: garden, work with plants, beautify the outdoors
- Decorate: beautify a setting [3]

Combining the lists of your five most fulfilling accomplishments and your five most significant abilities, write down your top five:

1. _____

2. _____

3. _____

4. _____

5. _____

Write your autobiography by recording your three most significant experiences at each age level. Consider the following types of experiences as you think about it.

- spiritual experiences (most meaningful decisions/times with God)
- painful experiences (problems, hurts, trials)
- educational experiences (favorite subjects, best teacher, where you learned the most)
- ministry experiences (opportunities to serve, witness)

Ages 1–12

1. _____
2. _____
3. _____

Ages 13–18

1. _____
2. _____
3. _____

Ages 19–22

1. _____
2. _____
3. _____

Ages 23 to present

1. _____
2. _____
3. _____

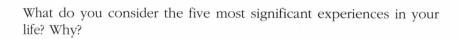
What do you consider the five most significant experiences in your life? Why?

1. _____
2. _____
3. _____
4. _____
5. _____

Write down a final list of your abilities and experiences:

1. _____
2. _____
3. _____
4. _____
5. _____
6. _____
7. _____
8. _____
9. _____
10. _____

Where is the primary place you can use these abilities and experiences for God's glory? [4]

_____

_____

_____

Give It *All*

What motivates you, and how does you give 100 percent?

2:27 P.M. I bolted out of class and ran to the gym for basketball practice. I arrived first and left last. From 2:45 until 5:00 every school day I practiced with the team. I wanted to hit more shots, make more free throws, win more sprints than anyone else on the team. With limited talent, my scrawny six-foot body was dwarfed in a big man's game. But I worked hard. I stayed after practice from 5:00 until 6:30 to work out on my own. In the summer I practiced eight hours every day and played in games three nights a week. I loved every minute of it. Nothing had a more beautiful sound than the ball bouncing on the floor and then swishing through the net. Often I wondered, What motivates me? Am I motivated for the right reasons?

Paul, the apostle, challenges us to wholehearted motivation in Colossians 3:23. What is his perspective?

_____

_____

_____

Whether we pursue photography, geometry, basketball, friendships, or hundreds of other interests, we need to invest every ounce of our energy into it for God's glory. That moves us toward our destiny.

Check the things that motivate you the most.

❑ Fun   ❑ Sports   ❑ Money   ❑ Acceptance
❑ Achievement   ❑ Friends   ❑ Hormones
❑ Parents' approval   ❑ Proving myself   ❑ Emotions

Yet something positive with the wrong motivation can negatively affect us.

Sharon's desire for achievement (a positive) combined with her fear of failure (a negative) almost ruined her. A highly skilled, successful All-State athlete, she broke down in sobs as she told me her story. To her it seemed like no matter how well she did, it was never quite good enough for her dad. She told me, "I can't ever please him. I can't take it anymore. I quit. I don't care."

The Lord rescued her out of her confusion and restored healthy motivation. That happened when she understood how to get properly motivated according to Colossians 3:23.

TOTAL MOTIVATION

When we pursue God's destiny for us, we can approach it only one way—with all of our hearts. That is total motivation!

Frequently I tell my wife, Carol, "Honey, I love you with all of my heart." But what if I told her, "Carol, I love you, but there are three other women I want to be with. I can only live with you . . . let's see . . . 25 percent of the time." Or what if I said, "Carol, I love you 95 percent of the time, but I want to see this other woman 5 percent of the time." Would you think I loved my wife? The only way to love her is with all of my heart.

We move away from total motivation when we focus on external behavior.

My daughter Katie played on her first basketball team at age eleven. The first game our girls got clobbered because all five of them hovered around the ball. After the game I told Katie I would teach her to get the ball out of that clump of girls and drive to the basket. Every day we worked on driving to the basket. I drilled her: "Get the ball and drive to the basket." The next Saturday the same gals in the same blue uniforms did the same thing they had done the week before—they hovered around the ball. I knew Katie would grab that ball and drive to the basket. But she didn't. I told Carol, "She is not driving to the basket." I called out to Katie, "Drive to the basket!" Still no response. I yelled it louder, "Drive to the basket!" It wasn't happening, so I yelled really loud as she was coming up the court, "Drive to the basket, Katie." She stopped in the middle of the court, put her hands on her hips, and yelled back, "Dad, I'm trying to drive to the basket." How embarrassing! External motivation at its finest failed!

Total motivation does not come from external behavior but from internal desire.

After a weekend of fever, our son, Scott, then fifteen, wasn't getting better. We took him to the hospital Monday morning. What started as a bad day got worse. By the end of the day the doctors had a tube in his lungs, fearful that he might not make it through the night. I called some men in our church to pray. As we gathered around his bed, the Lord gave us two prayers. One, that God's healing hand would touch him during the night in such a way that the doctors would know that it was God who did it, not medicine. Two, that the Lord would speak to Scott in his unconscious state about his life.

The next morning the nurse said, "Barry, it's like Scott's lung was black and now it is white." The doctors met later to discover what had caused such a radical change. When I went in the room, Scott was very animated, even though he could not talk because of the tube in his lungs. He wrote on a pad:

The other day on the news it said that the number of deaths related to the flu and pneumonia had reached epidemic proportions. When I found out about double pneumonia, it threw me for a loop. Lately my Christian walk has not been growing but at a standstill. Last night the Lord changed my view of Him, the world, and myself. He's put His vibrant Spirit wholeheartedly back into me. I woke up today praising the Lord just to be alive and exalting Him. Every time the nurses woke me up to do testing during the night, they said I had a great big smile on my face. I woke up singing, "This is the day the Lord has made." [Then he wrote in large letters] "PRAISE THE LORD!"

That experience internally motivated Scott to the degree that through high school he lived for Christ, and at Duke University he took on his fraternity as his mission. Now in medical school as a result of this experience, Scott and his wife are pursuing medical missions.

God creates total motivation internally when we want to please God "with all our hearts."

However, three "heartbreakers" want to steal that total motivation.

HÉARTBREAKER 1: WRONG MOTIVES

Many people are totally motivated but often with the wrong motives.

Jesus called these wrong motives "evil" in Mark 7:21–23. What wrong motives does He identify?

_____   _____   _____

_____   _____   _____

_____   _____   _____

We tend to think of the negative characteristics on this list as big-time sin. But all of these "big" sins begin with little motives. If we feed them, they grow until they suck godly motives out of us and pump evil desires into us. Then they control us.

God desires to turn evil motives into pure ones. He wants to clean up our unclean motives. How does that happen according to 1 John 1:9 and Ephesians 5:18?

_____

_____

_____

HÉARTBREAKER 2: MIXED MOTIVES

Other people fall into the trap of half-heartedness. Their motives aren't necessarily wrong, but they are mixed. They dabble at this and that, doing good things but not God's best thing. So they meander through life not sure why they do what they do.

The trap is wanting the best of both worlds. People want enough of God to have the good things that come with Jesus. But they desire what the world offers too. They think they can straddle the fence. Like the wishbone of a chicken, they begin to feel the pull. A person can only stand that pressure for so long.

The apostle James called these people "double-minded." What pictures does he use to describe them in James 1:1–8?

_____

_____

_____

But James turns the problem of "double-mindedness" into an opportunity for wholeheartedness. Look at what God does to get people out of the half-heartedness trap in James 4:6–8.

_____

_____

_____

According to James 1:6–8, what does God ask us to do? What do you need to do?

1. _____

2. _____

3. _____

In time God will purify our hearts through these steps. Instead of giving in to the tug toward half-heartedness, we will have a totally intense desire to please God.

HEARTBREAKER 3: WEAK MOTIVES

Fatigue, frustration, discouragement, burnout, exhaustion, stress, despair—a wave of circumstances can wash over even our pure motives and wipe us out.

When we become fainthearted, we may sound like this: "I have the 'spiritual blahs.' My Christian life has lost its focus. I am no longer motivated to live for Christ. I could not care less. What's wrong with me?"

What are some of the things that suck the energy out of you?

_____

_____

_____

What do we do when we get wiped out like that according to 2 Corinthians 4:16?

_____

_____

_____

That happened to Katie. A serious car wreck and a torn knee ligament within the span of a year overwhelmed her at first, but in the end they strengthened her motivation. These troubles helped her to "fix [her] eyes not on what is seen, but on what is unseen" (verse 18).

Going through these difficult challenges can purify our motives and lead us into total motivation.

The Heart Builder: Total Motivation

A receiver on a football team runs full speed downfield, jumps in the air with his arms extended while two 250-pound linebackers converge on his ribs. All of this is to catch a cheap piece of polished pigskin with Wilson written on it.

People give 100 percent for much less noble purposes than God's purpose.

But God wants that same kind of 100 percent wholeheartedness from us. How did Jesus describe it in Mark 12:30?

_____

_____

_____

How do you think you need to give 100 percent of your
• emotions?

_____

_____

_____

• personality?

_____

_____

_____

• intellect?

_____

_____

_____

- body?

_____

_____

_____

C. T. Studd, the most famous cricket player in nineteenth-century England, gave up his bright future in sports after Cambridge University. He had decided to go to China as a missionary with six other young men. They were known as the Cambridge Seven. When a group of students asked why, Studd replied, "If Jesus Christ be God and died for me, then no sacrifice can be too great for me to make for Him." Then he asked them: "Have you surrendered everything to Jesus Christ? Because if Jesus is not Lord of all, then He is not Lord at all."

How can we possess that kind of 100 percent wholehearted motivation found in Jesus Christ?

1. *Repent.* Let God's searchlight shine continually into every corner of your life to find anything that is not totally under His control

2. *Seek.* If we seek Him we will find Him. The more we find Him, the more we will want to seek Him. Pray this prayer: "Lord, today I am seeking to find You in every person and situation."

3. *Obey.* Obedience means taking action that goes against the grain of our personal desires. Make "Yes, Sir" your answer to the Lord no matter what the issue is.

4. *Serve.* Daily look for ways to give time, energy, and money for the cause of Christ.

5. *Rejoice.* Surrender doesn't mean somber. Instead of taking away the fun in life, He will give you more.

When we pursue motivation that "serves the Lord, not men" (Colossians 3:23), wholeheartedness will follow. That's another big step in living out God's destiny for our lives.

GET READY

1. To identify your motives take the Motives and Motivation Test on the next page.

2. Talk about it with your parents or a friend this week.

MOTIVES AND MOTIVATION TEST

Decide which of these issues hinders pure motives or stifles your motivation.

On a scale of 0–5 check (√) the ones you struggle with most. (0 is no struggle; 5 is total struggle). Make a list of your "Top Three" at the end of each section. Follow the instructions at the end of the test.

WRONG MOTIVES TEST

	0	1	2	3	4	5

Evil thoughts
Sexual immorality
    (messing with sex)
Theft (stealing, cheating)
Murder
    (hateful thoughts or actions
    intended to hurt someone)
Adultery
    (sex outside of marriage)
Greed (materialism)
Malice (hatred)
Deceit (lying, cheating)
Lewdness (obscene language
    or actions)
Envy (jealousy)
Slander (gossip)
Arrogance (pride)
Folly (party animal)

TOP THREE:

    1. _____

    2. _____

    3. _____

MIXED MOTIVES TEST

In this section make a list of two under each question, and then proceed with the instructions.

<u>   0   1   2   3   4   5 </u>

1. What do you worry about most?
   1. _____
   2. _____

2. On what do you spend most of your money?
   1. _____
   2. _____

3. In what do you place your security?
   1. _____
   2. _____

4. What makes you feel important?
   1. _____
   2. _____

5. What do you daydream about?
   1. _____
   2. _____

TOP THREE:

   1. _____

   2. _____

   3. _____

WEAK MOTIVES TEST

Which of these pressures cause you to lose motivation?

	0	1	2	3	4	5

Negative attitudes
Wrong priorities
Burnout
No time with God
Negative talk
Disappointment
Guilt
Overcommitment
Poor eating habits
Broken relationship
No time with family
Fatigue
No exercise
Work stress
Fear

TOP THREE:

1. _____
2. _____
3. _____

TOTAL MOTIVATION TEST

Choose the three you struggle with the most out of the total list and write them in the blanks below.

_____

_____

_____

Write out a specific plan to turn negative motivation into positive motivation.

_____

_____

_____

Walk through the steps on page 77 to write your plan.

1. _____

My plan: _____

2. _____

My plan: _____

3. _____

My plan: _____

If you marked any categories in the 4–5 range, talk to a Christian friend, your pastor, or a counselor to help you get these under God's control.

Aim at the Target

What is your life purpose, and how do you discover it?

He went deer hunting at every opportunity. His girlfriend had never gone. She insisted that he take her. He told her, "It will be cold, dark, and the briers will scratch you." She persisted. They went. He was right. The morning was cold and dark, and the briers did scratch her. When they got to a clearing, he showed her how to shoot the gun. Then he put her on the deer stand and went off through the woods. About a hundred yards away, he heard bang, bang, bang! He hustled back through the brush, got back to the edge of the clearing, and saw his girlfriend pointing her gun at a man. He was standing with his hands in the air. She was yelling, "That's my deer. That's my deer. You get away from my deer." The man yelled, "OK, lady, OK, just let me get the saddle and the bridle off."

THIS WOMAN DID NOT KNOW WHAT TO AIM FOR! As we zero in on our purpose in life, we want to make certain that we aim at the right target.

TAKING AIM

An ad in *Newsweek* stated: "Last year Americans traveled 350 billion miles and never found what they were looking for. . . ."

Without purpose, we are like the turnpike close to my home in West Virginia. It's the turnpike that "starts nowhere and ends nowhere." Without purpose we're traveling, but going nowhere.

Our purpose is our target. If we miss it, we miss the entire reason for our existence.

How would you describe "purpose"?

_____

_____

_____

Our purpose:

- drives us
- keeps us awake at night
- wakes us up in the morning
- causes us to jump out of bed with enthusiasm
- gets us excited
- expresses our hopes and dreams
- is our North Star
- is worth dying for

> **Without purpose we're traveling, but going nowhere.**

Even though most people don't know what they are aiming for, that does not have to be true of you. You can locate the target, take aim, and fire!

THE TARGET

Only one life, twill soon be past;
Only what's done for Christ will last.

Soon after I began to follow Christ, someone sent me this message on a card. As a young Christian it helped me target my purpose.

The apostle Paul knew the target. According to Philippians 3:8 what was it?

_____

_____

_____

With intense focus he expressed his life purpose again in Philippians 3:10. What was it?

_____

_____

_____

Let's start at the outer edge of the target and work our way to the bull's-eye. Once we know our general purpose, we can more easily discover our unique, specific purpose.

To Know Him

To what lengths would you go to meet a superstar? Knowing Jesus is a million times more valuable than meeting Michael Jordan. Why?

Blaise Pascal, one of the greatest scientists and philosophers of all time, wrote, "Apart from Jesus Christ, we know not what our life is, nor our death, nor God, nor ourselves."[1]

That puts a high premium on knowing Christ. But what does it mean?

"To know" is more than

- learning a few simple facts about Jesus
- reading the Bible occasionally
- having some vague religious experience
- joining a church

"To know" means an intimate, personal relationship. Closeness, communication, warmth, and love are part of knowing Christ. That is why when Jesus called His disciples, they considered knowing Him of such value that they left everything and followed Him (Matthew 4:20).

> As Leonardo da Vinci painted "The Last Supper," a crowd watched over his shoulder. He was working on the fruit on the table. When he saw that the crowd had their eyes glued on the fruit, angrily he stroked across the fruit, obliterating it. Pointing to the face of Christ, he said, "Don't look down there, look up here."

Aim at knowing Jesus. He is the target.

To Make Him Known

Asked how he could make such beautiful figures out of a plain block of marble, a famous sculptor replied: "I picture a tiger in my mind, then I hammer and chisel on that block of marble until everything is gone but tiger."

That's what the apostle Paul had in mind when he said we are to become "like Him" (Philippians 3:10).

✳ How do you think "becoming like him" makes Him known to others?

_____

_____

_____

In Philippians 3:10 what two ways does God use to help us become like "Him"?

1. _____

2. _____

Through the power of the resurrection (God's hammer) and the fellowship of His suffering (God's chisel), He works in us and on us until we are transformed to look like Him.

The power of His resurrection. Because Christ lives in us, we have the same power living in us now that raised Jesus from the dead. Through that power we can change to become like Him.

To get some idea of our power to change, compare the resurrection power to a nuclear bomb. One nuclear bomb can destroy the world 267 times. Yet all the nuclear bombs in the world do not begin to demonstrate the power that it took to raise Jesus from the dead. That unique power can help us live in a way that reflects Jesus Christ and makes Him known to others. Through the power of the resurrection we can know God's purpose for us and accomplish it.

The fellowship of His sufferings. People love power. But suffering never draws a large crowd. Yet sharing in Christ's sufferings comes as part of the "purpose package." "Why doesn't God just take away my problems so I can be happy?" Because suffering transforms us into the image of Christ. When life is a bed of roses, we tend to lose the intensity of wanting to know Christ. But when pressure pursues us, we turn to Him. That is why the apostle Paul called it a gift "granted to you" (Philippians 1:29).

Everything I touched when I was growing up turned into success. Then in my first year of college everything I touched seemed to fail. My grandmother, who was my closest friend, died just before I left for college. No matter how hard I tried, I didn't do well in academics or athletics. On Homecoming Weekend my date stood me up. All of my friends came in drunk. I woke up that Saturday morning and stared out the window with a deep emptiness. For the first time in my life these questions flooded my mind: "Who am I?" "What am I doing here?" "Where am I going?" Even though it took several months to discover the answers, it was out of that sense of futility, my first suffering, that I launched out on the journey to find my life purpose.

Cancer, the death of a loved one, and rejection in a relationship chip self off of us and create a God-shape in us.

✳ What promise does God make to us about difficulties in our lives in Romans 8:28?

_____

_____

_____

✳ What two conditions does God put on the promise?

1. _____

2. _____

✳ According to Romans 8:29 what is God doing as a result of our difficulties?

_____

_____

_____

God wants to use difficulties and problems in our lives to make us more and more like Him! The more we become like Him the more we fulfill our purpose.

THE BULL'S-EYE

Now that we have hit the target—to know Him and make Him known—let's take aim at our specific purpose.

Years ago Dianna Ross of "The Supremes" fame phrased the question well about our purpose.

Do you know where you're going to?

To express the question more graphically, when people gather around your casket to pay their last respects, what do you want them to say about you?

Your life can be represented by a straight line that has as its origin your birth and an arrow on the opposite end indicating the unknown time of your death. None of us know how long we will have in this life, but let's say you have lived close to twenty years and you have approximately fifty years left. Here is the question: When you come to the end of those fifty years, and you have nothing but death to look forward to and nothing but memories to look back upon, what will you need to see for you to conclude, "My life was a success"?[2]

A fun evening is not sitting around thinking about when we are going to die. However, to discover our life purpose, we have to begin there. "All planning begins at the end," someone said. When we call a travel agent to plan a trip, what is the first question they ask? "What is your final destination?" Thinking about our final destination will help us determine our purpose now.

What is your unique, specific life purpose? For an example, I have included my son Jonathan's purpose statement:

> **My purpose in life is to love God with a heart of gratitude, a soul of obedience, and a mind of dependence on Him, and to love others as myself by serving.**

Mack Douglas summarizes the significance and value of discovering our purpose: "What is the difference in one man and another? Here's a man who is dynamically, enthusiastically, vibrantly alive. Everything he does is charged with power. Here's another who droops, drags and meanders through mere existence. The difference is purpose. There is amazing power in purpose."[3]

GET READY

1. Ask yourself the Five Questions on page 90, praying for the Lord to reveal His specific, unique purpose to you.

2. Follow the Five Instructions on page 90 in writing your purpose statement. Make sure you go through the three stages of writing it to avoid getting yourself bogged down. Keep working on it until you come up with your final purpose statement.

3. Share your purpose statement with at least one other person. Get feedback on whether or not it hits the bull's-eye of your uniqueness.

   Remember: Don't try to do all of this in one sitting. Work on it some each day until you are comfortable with it. This takes time and effort. Take the time and put in the effort. It will help you the rest of your life.

THE PURPOSE DISCOVERY EXERCISE

These specific guidelines will help you discover your purpose.

Five Questions

Ask yourself these specific, penetrating questions.[4] Jot down notes on a spearate piece of paper as you think through each one. Pray, asking God to reveal His specific purpose to you.

1. Why do I exist?
2. When I die, what do I want my friends and family to say about me? (What do I want my epitaph to say?)
3. How am I totally unique?
4. What do I feel deeply burdened about?
5. What does God want me to do?

Five Instructions

Using the Five Questions as background, follow these instructions to write your purpose.

1. Pray: "Lord show me Your purpose for me."
2. Make your purpose statement broad.
3. Realize that this statement should span your entire life.
4. Understand that you do not have to express end results or measurable goals. That will come later.
5. Write your purpose statement using the following three steps.

   - Write your statement any way you want. Make it as long as you like. Let this flow. Don't get uptight thinking that if you write something, you will never be able to change it.
   - Write three key words. From what you wrote above identify the three action verbs that express what you want to do with your life.
   - Write the final statement. Using the three key words above, express your purpose as one, brief, clear, easy-to-understand sentence. Remember: It should fit on a T-shirt!

Once you write your purpose statement to your satisfaction, type it. Keep it with you all the time. Memorize it. Verbalize it to others. Carry it in your wallet. Place it in the front of your notebook.

Know Which End Is Up

What are your values, and how do you define them?

Rod and I were to fly from Oklahoma City to Sante Fe on a commercial flight. As we stood in the hall discussing our plans, a fellow we knew, overhearing our conversation, offered to fly us in his small, private plane. Never having flown in a small plane, both of us looked at each other with that "no way" look. But that is not what came out. "I will if you will," I blurted. "Well, I will if you will," he challenged. We went.

At the airport the wind was blowing so hard that when our pilot unlatched the plane it whipped around like a wild dog on a leash. When we loaded the luggage, the tires kept getting lower and lower! We had to manually turn the propellers to get it started. I wanted out!

Instead we got in, Rod in the back and me in the front. We sput . . . sput . . . sputtered down the taxiway. About halfway down the runway the thought hit me: *This is nothing but a go-cart with wings.* Before I could process that, a clump of trees was staring us in the face. I thought, We're dead. At the last moment the pilot pulled back the stick, and we cleared the trees by inches.

Higher and higher we went, until it seemed like we could see all of Oklahoma. Now more fascinated than fearful, I asked lots of questions. Rod was quiet in the back. Then the pilot asked me, "Do you want to fly the plane?" Before I could respond, he flipped the steering wheel in front of me. Vrooooom! The plane veered to the right. Vrooooom! The plane veered to the left. By the time I got control, Rod was "white-knuckling" in the back.

Then moments later a large cloud appeared. I asked about going around it. Under it? Would you believe over it? "No— through it." I knew it was only a cloud. Nothing more than condensed water, I recalled from eighth grade science. My conscious mind was saying, "Cloud," but my subconscious mind kept shouting, "Wall!" I pictured myself becoming a grease spot on impact. Sure enough, we eased into the cloud. I couldn't see anything. We were at it again. Vrooooom! Vroooom! After the third or fourth "vrooooom," I took a quick glance to the back. White as a sheet, Rob grabbed for the "vomit bag."

Grabbing the controls as the plane lurched, the pilot muttered, "St. Clair, you don't know which end is up." The rest of the trip he flew by instruments.

FLYING BY THE INSTRUMENTS

THAT PLANE RIDE WAS LIKE LIFE. As we go places we have never been and do things we have never done, our lives can easily veer out of control. We mutter, "I don't know which end is up." But if we do know which end is up and navigate by the instrument panel of our values, not only will we avoid crashing, we can move toward God's destiny for us.

What is a value, according to the apostle Paul in Colossians 3:1–2?

_____

_____

_____

_____

> **Values keep us on course when the pressure is on to behave otherwise.**

What we live for and think about is what we value. When we value something, we honor it, we love it, and we hold it in high esteem. A value is a quality, object, or person that we look at and say, "That is important."

For followers of Christ, Jesus is our "core value." According to Colossians 3:3, why is He the center of our value system?

_____

_____

_____

_____

We fly by His "things above" instrument panel. He keeps us on course when the pressure is on to behave otherwise.

What we valued before our life was "hidden with Christ in God" should be totally different from what we value now. Why, according to Colossians 3:1–2?

_____

_____

_____

_____

The more we set our hearts and minds on what is on God's heart and mind, the more our values will change to reflect His values.

My friend, Hani, a brilliant, young medical doctor from a Middle Eastern country shared his faith with a Moslem. (Due to the danger of being a Christian in his country, neither his real name or country can be given.) Arrested and put in prison for this, they placed Hani in a cell with another man. The cell was only large enough for the two of them to stand. Hani contracted a kidney disease and almost died. At any point he could have renounced Jesus Christ and been freed. Instead, he remained in prison almost to the point of death. Only the assassination of the country's president made it possible for him to go free. When I asked him what he learned from his prison experience, he replied, "I learned that only two things are important in life: to love God and love people." Clearly knowing his values before prison kept him from giving in to the pressure, and his prison experience served to intensify and deepen his core values.

We don't have to go to prison to discover or deepen our values. But as we "set our minds on things above," God will focus and fashion our values around Jesus.

VERTIGO VALUES

Flying can easily cause vertigo. Even pilots get it. Vertigo means losing all sense of where we are because we get dizzy and everything feels like it is spinning. Our culture has "vertigo values." We are spinning out of control.

Appropriately situated in the context of an illustration of undressing and dressing, the apostle Paul gives a partial list of "vertigo values" in Colossians 3:5–9. Just as a person takes off dirty clothes to take a bath, we need to take these off:

_____

_____

_____

These "earthly things" no longer have value to us. Do you still "wear" any of these? Which ones?

_____

_____

_____

Take them off! Picture yourself dropping them to the floor like dirty, sweaty, stinking clothes.

VITAL VALUES

Our purpose points us to our destination, but our values determine our behavior on the way.

Upon landing our plane in Santa Fe on that fateful day, the pilot grinned and exclaimed, "Cheated death again." When a plane crashes, almost always it is attributed to "pilot error." If the pilot operates the plane correctly, you will get to your destination. If he doesn't, you're dead.

Our values are like that.

When we have values like the ones listed in Colossians 3:12–16, then those values create vitality, life, in us. Without them we become dead, lifeless. Following Paul's illustration of undressing and dressing (verses 9–10), we see that once we get the dirty clothes off, then we put the clean clothes on. We clothe ourselves with

_____

_____

_____

These "things above" have great value. Put them on! Picture yourself taking each one off the hanger and putting it on to wear. Now you are stylin', lookin' good from God's point of view.

FINDING CONGRUITY

"How do I determine which values I need for my life? How do I decide which ones are important?" you ask.

> While speaking in St. Simons Island, Georgia, I met Bill, a businessman who helps the Lithuanian government buy American planes. He invited me to take a plane tour over the islands. That sounded like fun. When I met him at his office, I was expecting to take the shiny twin engine plane in the hangar. He took me out to the seven Lithuanian planes he had bought recently. He got excited about us flying one of the old "red and white tin cans" with cotton cloth bi-wings. Four of us pushed the propeller ten times to get it started. The instrument panel was in Russian. The seats looked like nailed down kitchen chairs. We flew with the back door open!
>
> When we got up, Bill let me fly. I took it down to six feet above the beach—intentionally. I loved it. It was the unique highlight of my summer. I got so excited about that little trip because I value adventure highly.

That experience brought together a value (adventure) and the application of that value (the plane ride). This is called the *principle of congruity*. That means the coming together of what you believe (a value) and how you perform (an action).[1]

We can diagram it like this.

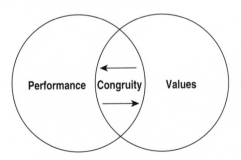

The more our values and our performance overlap, the higher the degree of congruity. The more congruity we have in our lives, the more fun we have and the more we live out our destiny.

We can operate on four different levels of values, which are described below. But when our "core value" is Jesus Christ (Colossians 3:3), congruity is at its highest level.

1. *Instincts.* This person lives by natural urges, seeking to satisfy base desires.

2. *Approval.* Values are determined by the approval of others—family, church, community, friends.

3. *Conscience.* Behavior adjusts to conscience. This person has a moral sense of right and wrong.

4. *Christian.* This person utilizes his conscience for guidance and the Holy Spirit to empower him or her. Here a person becomes most complete, realizing the divinely ordained potential of his life. Here he or she experiences the highest degree of congruity.[2]

Understanding these four levels shows us the significance of biblical values. On the Christian level not only can we know the highest values, but also we have the supernatural power to act on those values so that what we value and what we do are in congruity.

GET READY

1. Work through each step of the Values Investigation at the end of the chapter until you have clearly expressed your values in writing.

2. Verbally express those to your parents or a friend. Included is an example of one student's values.

MY VALUES:

1. *Jesus Christ.* Spend time studying about Him and praying to Him in order to understand His love and become more like Him.

2. *Family.* Love my family so others may see Christ in us.

3. *Friends.* Encourage my friends in order to help each one reach his or her full potential.

4. *Ministry.* Take opportunities to encourage other Christians and share the gospel with non-Christians.

5. *Academics.* Study hard to maximize my academic potential.

6. Athletics. Offer my body as a worshipful sacrifice to God by training diligently.

VALUES INVESTIGATION

Follow these steps to determine your values.

1. Brainstorm possible values.

   Make a list of all of your possible values. Then look through them to see if any of them could combine with others.[2.]

2. Understand the following values grid.

Picture your values like this:

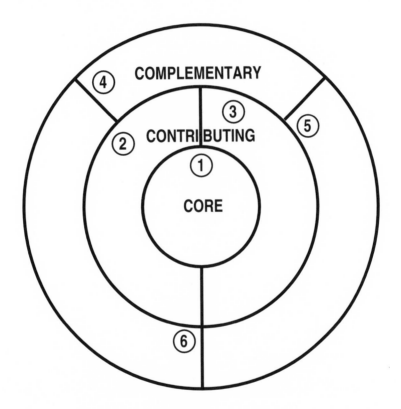

Ask yourself these questions:

- What is my *core* value? The most important one to you.
- What values *contribute* to my core value? The two values that are next most important to you.
- What values *complement* my first three values? The three values that you consider most important after the first three.

3. Choose your final list of six values.

   Determine the six values that you deem most important, then decide your one core value, your two contributing values, and your three complimentary values.

   1. _____

   2. _____

   3. _____

   4. _____

   5. _____

   6. _____

4. Define each value as an action statement.

   Begin the statement with an action verb, and then define how the value will be expressed. (For example: Family. Love my family by serving the.)

   _____

   _____

   _____

   _____

   _____

   _____

5. Identify any incongruity.

   Write down any areas where your behavior does not match up to your values. Ask the Lord to bring your behavior in line with your values. Take whatever steps He shows you.

   _____

   _____

   _____

   _____

chapter 11

Run for the Finish Line

What are your goals, and how do you set them?

Finish the Atlanta Marathon in less than three hours! To cover 26.2 miles in that time would qualify me for the Boston Marathon. Could I reach that goal?

Even before I started, I almost self-destructed. With all of my training and preparation, I forgot one small detail. In all of the excitement, I left my race number on the counter at home. I didn't have time to go back and get it. I called my wife, Carol. In trying to find it, she woke up everyone at 6:30 a.m. on Thanksgiving Day. The hunt was on. And they found it. By then there was no time to get it to me. The race officials told me that I could start the race without my number, but I couldn't finish without it. Whew!

My father-in-law had taken me to the race. We worked it out for him to meet me with the number at a certain point. By the time we arranged everything and I hurried to the starting line, the race had begun. Not only did I not have time to warm up, but I began the race forty-five seconds late.

With all of those glitches and distractions, I could have quit before the race began.

Up to mile 20 I was ahead of my pace of 6:30 per mile and I had my number. Then it began to rain and I "hit the wall." With shoes that felt like they weighed twenty pounds apiece, and cold rain that caused my legs to cramp, my body was yelling at me: "STOP!" Others were stopping, why didn't I? Often I've asked myself, "Why did you keep on running?" I had a goal! I didn't want to give up on my lifetime goal of running in the Boston Marathon. That caused me to press on. Using every ounce of energy I had, I finished in two hours and fifty-seven minutes. I reached the goal!

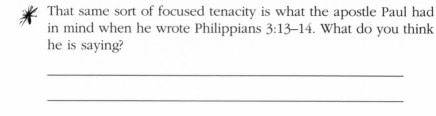
 That same sort of focused tenacity is what the apostle Paul had in mind when he wrote Philippians 3:13–14. What do you think he is saying?

_____

_____

_____

Following Jesus is like a race—a marathon. Only those who have their goals clearly in mind will "press on toward the goal to win the prize." How do we do that?

CONNECTING WITH OUR PURPOSE

Our endless number of activities and "to do" lists cause our lives to look like this:

"There's a lot of verbal 'fog' floating around in Christian circles because of fuzzy ill-defined purposes and goals. We talk about giving God glory, taking the gospel into the world, and living God-honoring lives. But as long as such statements remain undefined, they are useless."[1]

Without goals that connect to our purpose, we are left with total confusion.

However when we set goals based on our life purpose and values, then we can be confident that every decision is taking us in the right direction. Then our lives can look like this:

LIFE PURPOSE

 What does the apostle Paul say in Philippians 3:12 about staying focused on our purpose?

_____

_____

_____

In order to run the race we must connect our goals with our purpose. For years I knew this must be true, but I didn't know how to make that connection. Now I know, and I want to show you.

OUR NEED TO ACHIEVE

Struggling with reaching his purpose and goals, the apostle Paul made a confession in Philippians 3:13–14. What was it?

_____

_____

_____

What struggles have you had in setting and reaching goals?

_____

_____

_____

People seem to fall into one of two ditches on the road to goal setting.

Hyper-goal setters. Carried away with changing the world by the end of this week, hyper-goal setters set themselves on a burnout course. Unrealistic and inflexible goals dull their sensitivity to people. Driving overachievers quickly get their lives out of balance.

Non-goal setters. Not wanting to get out of their comfort zone, non-goal setters don't see the need for setting goals. Satisfied with the status quo, they don't like to be challenged to press on. They like their lives just like they are.

Some may be stalled on the side of the road for other reasons:

- No one has shown me the importance of goal setting.
- I don't know how to approach it.
- I don't like to write things down.
- It is too much trouble.
- They haven't taken the time.
- I failed in the past and feel I would never reach the goal.

Whatever the reason, we miss out on the balance that God desires. Each personality type will respond to goal setting differently. However, we can say with certainty that God desires everyone to enter into balanced goal setting in order to achieve God's purpose for our lives. We must set goals if we are going to "win the prize."

> At seventy my dad retired, sort of. He dreamed about buying some land on the interstate to build a motel. He didn't need the money, the hassle, or something else to do. But he felt like God gave him the vision for it and the ability to do it. So he borrowed the money, purchased the land, got the construction crew, and built a motel. He had never been in the motel business before! Why did he build it? He had a dream, a goal. Even past seventy years old, he never stifled his need to achieve—to press on toward the goal.

When we set goals we benefit for many reasons.[2]

1. *We avoid the tyranny of the urgent.* Without goals, daily urgencies overwhelm us so that we rarely get to the really important things.

2. *We get revitalized.* People with goals generally have tremendous energy reserves. They create energy as they set systematic goals that move them toward their life purpose.

3. *We accomplish more.* Only three percent of all people have goals written down. Ten percent more have them in their heads. Eighty-seven percent drift through life with no definite goals. The three percent accomplish fifty to one hundred times more in their lifetimes than those ten percent who have the goals in their heads. And they achieve infinitely more than those who have no goals.[3]

4. *We experience fulfillment.* Personally, I have discovered that almost every time I get discouraged I can trace it to having lost sight of my goals or having too many goals. One of the outstanding benefits of setting goals is personal happiness.

5. *We build confidence.* Without goals we don't know how to proceed. Like walking in a dark room, we run into walls and hit our shins. We get confused about where we are and where we are supposed to go. Goal setting turns the light on so we can see to move through the room with confidence.

12 QUESTIONS

 Find the phrase in Philippians 3:13 that expresses Dawson Trotman's thoughts.

_____

_____

_____

> **This one thing**
>
> **I do;**
>
> **not forty things**
>
> **I dabble at.**
>
> **Dawson Trotman, founder of the Navigators.**

How do we set specific goals that move us toward our purpose?

* Write one goal you want to accomplish.

_____

_____

Now ask yourself these questions to see if you set it correctly.

1. *Do I understand what a goal is?* According to Webster a goal is "an end that one strives for." The goal is the finish line.

2. *Have I written the goal?* Since we remember only 10 percent of what we hear, but retain 70 percent of what we hear and write, it makes sense that our goals will be clearer if we write them. Writing keeps it before us to remind us where we are headed.

3. *Have I set the right goal?* Disappointment results when we set the wrong goals. A wrong goal satisfies our own selfish desires, leaving God and others out of the picture. But setting the right goal and achieving it honors God and others. We can ask ourselves, "Does this goal please the Lord?"

4. *Is this God's goal for me?* Praying through the goal allows us to determine if the goal fits our purpose and values. Imagine how much time, energy, and effort we can save by only pursuing God's goals for us.

5. *Is my goal big enough?* Dawson Trotman gave a profound challenge, "Why pray for peanuts when God wants to give us continents!" Small goals stifle our faith, our vision, and our walk with Christ. Let's allow our goals to stretch our faith. Let's dream big dreams—big enough that unless God comes through we are doomed to failure.

6. *Have I established a realistic goal?* On the flip side we have to ask ourselves if the goal is doable. No one can be an astronaut

if he has never been to college. Or to bring it closer to home, a person cannot get an A in a course if she has not cracked a book all semester. Unrealistic goals overwhelm and demotivate us. Yet realistic goals set within realistic time frames bring success.

7. *Can I visualize the goal?* Picture yourself reaching your goal. What do you see? Is it worth achieving? Visualizing the goal will program your subconscious mind so that your actions will follow what your mind has seen. Right thinking always precedes right acting.

8. *Have I committed myself to the goal?* Ask yourself: "In light of other goals, can I realistically commit myself to this particular goal?"

9. *What barriers do I face?* Every worthy goal will face obstacles. The more lofty our goals the greater the obstacles. But we will willingly jump over these hurdles when we know that we are pursuing God's goals. Allow for obstacles without getting discouraged and quitting.

10. *Have I broken down the goal into simple, reachable steps?* The old adage goes, "How do you eat an elephant? One bite at a time." We won't accomplish the goal all in one day. But we need to do something to reach it every day. We need to break our goals into bite-sized chunks.

11. *Who will hold me accountable for this goal?* People live sloppy lives when no one holds them accountable. But when we are accountable, we help each other set goals, keep on track, and feel encouraged when we want to quit.

12. *When do I set my other goals?* We find time to do what is important to us. Carve out a few hours one afternoon or a few minutes every day over the next week to write your goals.

THE PRIZE

The result? The "prize."

> When I finished the marathon, the officials put a medal around my neck—the prize. I had qualified to run the Boston Marathon. (That's another story.)

When we finish life's race, having pursued God's goals for us, He will place around our necks "the prize." Like Paul we will be able to say, "I have fought the good fight, I have finished the race, . . . Now there is in store for me the crown of righteousness" (2 Tim. 4:7–8).

GET READY

1. On a piece of paper, write your goals using the outlines on page 106.
   - Set at least one goal under each category. Make each one personal (yours not somebody else's), practical (realistic), and measurable (specific).
   - Under each goal write down the steps you'll need to take to help you get there.
   - Set your One Year Goals.
   - Then use your One Year Goals to set your Monthly Goals.
   - Take plenty of time to work on this. Don't feel like you have to finish it all in one week.
2. Share your goals with your parents or a friend.

   Here are my son Jonathan's goals to give you an example.

Yearly Goals

Spiritual
1. Spend thirty minutes every morning for Bible study and prayer
2. Spend thirty minutes every evening for Scripture memorization

Mental
1. Make a 4.0 for senior year
2. Read one book a month

Physical
1. Run at least five days a week
2. Get at least eight hours of sleep a night

Social
1. Seek out a few specific people to invest myself into
2. Service anyone in need

Family
1. Do not procrastinate; do things right when they ask
2. Have a good attitude no matter what

Monthly Goals

Spiritual
1. Study Ephesians

Mental
1. Read Spiritual Disciplines for the Christian Life

Physical
1. Run at least twenty-five miles a week

Social
1. Focus my eyes on serving others

Family
1. Take out the trash without being asked

GOAL SETTING EXERCISE

MY LIFE PURPOSE

_____

_____

_____

_____

_____

_____

ONE YEAR GOALS

(Luke 2:52)
- Spiritual (quiet time, prayer, Bible study, accountability/ discipleship, outreach, church, ministry)
- Mental (school, grades, reading)
- Physical (exercise, diet, sleep)
- Social (friends, dating standards, activities)
- Family (parents, brothers, and sisters)
- Job/Finances (hours worked, money earned, possessions, tithe)

MONTHLY GOALS

(Luke 2:52)
- Spiritual (quiet time, prayer, Bible study, accountability/ discipleship, outreach, church, ministry)
- Mental (school, grades, reading)
- Physical (exercise, diet, sleep)
- Social (friends, dating standards, activities)
- Family (parents, brothers, and sisters)
- Job/Finances (hours worked, money earned, possessions, tithe)

chapter 12

Watch the Clock

What time do you have, and how do you use it?

Seventh grade PE. Basketball, dodgeball, tumbling and running. Anything was better than classes with books, even though our gym didn't have a shower. But one activity I hated—rope climbing. Gripping the rope tightly with my hands then wrapping my feet around the rope, I would start to climb. With hand over fist pushing against the law of gravity, I felt the strength go out of my arms. When I checked my progress, I had only climbed eight feet and had twenty to go. I couldn't do it. One day, after repeated efforts, I made it. I got so excited when I touched the top that I slid down quickly, letting the rope run through my fingers. When I reached the floor, my hands looked like one big, raw, juicy blister.

OUR STRUGGLE WITH TIME PARALLELS that rope climb. Getting time under control is like the constant strain of pulling up on the rope. Yet just at the point when we conquer it, like a slick rope, it slides through our fingers.

Time, unlike money, cannot be saved, only spent. No saving for a rainy day; we must spend every second *now*. Yesterday is a canceled check. Tomorrow is a promissory note. Today must be spent wisely.[1]

The average American who lives seventy years spends his or her time like this:

- 23 years sleeping
- 19 years working
- 9 years playing
- 6 years traveling
- 6 years eating
- 4 years sick
- 2 years dressing
- 1 year in church

We spend 69/70ths of life on temporal things and only 1/70th pursuing our eternal destiny.

Time is ticking by. To understand how to use it wisely, picture a clock with three hands ticking. When we understand how these three hands work, we will know how to use our time to pursue our destiny.

Contrasting wisdom and foolishness in Ephesians 5:15–17, the apostle Paul told us how to use the three ticking hands to watch the clock. What did he say to do?

1. _____

2. _____

3. _____

THE HOUR HAND—LOOK AT HOW YOU LIVE

Ephesians 5:15 can read, "Look at how you conduct your life and spend your time." We can do that best by contrasting how we look at time with how God looks at it.

The White Rabbit

We approach time like the white rabbit in Lewis Carroll's *Alice in Wonderland*. Always in a hurry, the white rabbit would pull out his watch and pop down a hole whenever Alice tried to get close to him. Running away from himself and others, he would exclaim, "Oh my ears and whiskers, how late it is getting!" Like the white rabbit we find ourselves always in a hurry. Sometimes we are running away from ourselves and our relationships. Sometimes our circumstances force us into an out-of-breath use of time.

> **Dost thou love life? Then do not squander time, For that's the stuff life is made of.**
>
> **Sir Walter Scott [3]**

The Time Monster

Even though we panic about time, we waste tremendous amounts of it. "Where did all of my time go?" we wonder. The "Time Monster" seems to steal time from us.

Looking at this list, circle your top three time wasters in each category.[2]

SELF-IMPOSED	OTHERS IMPOSED
Writing off responsibilities	Interruptions
Not making a decision	Telephone
Losing things	Family problems
Television	Poor communication
Lack of goals	Not enough help
Lack of planning	Unsure about responsibility
Day dreaming	Changing priorities
Wrong priorities	Waiting for people
Not listening	Commuting time
Emotional upset	Negative attitudes
Poor organization	Bogged down in detail work
Lack of self-discipline	People talk too long

TIMING IS EVERYTHING

By contrast, when we look at the clock from God's perspective, we find a much different approach than either panic or waste.

1. *Life is brief.* Get God's insight on the brevity of life from Psalm 39:4–5.

   _____

   _____

   _____

2. *Use time wisely.* Write in your own words what that means from Psalm 90:12.

   _____

   _____

   _____

3. *Accomplish your destiny.* God will give us enough time to accomplish everything in our destiny. What is the viewpoint of Ecclesiastes 3:1 on this?

   _____

   _____

   _____

Neither panic nor waste are options for us because "He [God] has made everything beautiful in its time" (Ecclesiastes 3:11).

Timing is everything! But only when it is in God's hands. Not only does He control the tick of the clock, the writer of Ecclesiastes went so far as to say that "He has . . . set eternity in the hearts of men" (Ecclesiastes 3:11). With the time He has given us, He will accomplish His destiny for us.

THE MINUTE HAND—MAKE EVERY MINUTE COUNT

When the apostle Paul wrote of "making the most of every opportunity" (Ephesians 5:16), he gave us the minute hand on the clock. What does that verse say to you?

_____

_____

_____

The apostle Paul had two great ideas about how to use time wisely.

1. *Make every minute count.* Let's picture ourselves in the grocery store filling a cart with our favorite food. The same principle applies to time: putting into every minute the best stuff we can.

2. *Redeem the time.* After I eat at one of my favorite restaurants so many times using my frequent diner card, I can redeem it for a free meal. If we use our time for God's purposes, He will redeem it. He will multiply our use of time for His glory.

The greatest example of making every minute count and redeeming the time was Jesus. It was no coincidence that He had completed His life's mission by age thirty-three. Even though He had a brief life span, He was never in a hurry, in a panic, or burned out. Because of the *quality* of the way He spent His time, He didn't need as much *quantity* to fulfill His destiny. Because Jesus lives in us, we can have that same balanced approach.

No one has any more or less time than anyone else. It's all in the way we choose to use it. Each one of us has 1,440 minutes a day, 168 hours a week. Of those hours we will

sleep	56 hours
eat and dress	20 hours
work	40 hours
travel	8 hours
TOTAL	124 hours
OPTIONAL	44 hours

What could we do with forty-four hours a week used wisely?

Make every minute count!

THE SECOND HAND— CONTROL THE TIME

By now we know we need to make adjustments in the use of our time.

In Ephesians 5:17, what happens when "the spirits" are in control?

_____

_____

_____

_____

In verse 18, what happens when "the Spirit" is in control?

_____

_____

_____

_____

> The distinction between a successful and mediocre existence is in those surplus minutes and hours which are either frittered away or afforded miserly care.[4]

Fools, like the drunk in verse 18, are out of control. Because they squander what they have, they miss out on God's will for their lives. On the other hand, the wise who are controlled by the Spirit make prudent decisions about the use of their resources, including time. Because of that, they walk in God's will.

> Though I am
>
> always in haste,
>
> I am never
>
> in a hurry
>
> because I never
>
> undertake more
>
> work than I can
>
> go through
>
> with calmness
>
> of spirit.
>
> —John Wesley

How do we make wise time decisions? *Say no graciously.* "I am convinced that the most difficult word to pronounce is not Zaanannim (Joshua 19:33) or Hazzelelponi (1 Chronicles 4:3). This word is even harder to say than 'The sixth sick sheik's sixth sheep is sick.' The word . . . is 'no.'"[5]

Charles Spurgeon said it more directly: "Learn to say no; . . . When you don't say no you make promises you can't keep, go to meetings that are not necessary and waste time in many inappropriate activities."[6]

Saying no is tough! We want people to like us. We think the need is urgent. We think we are indispensable. "It can't be done without me." But we must remember: Every time we say no to one thing we can say yes to something else!

Let's not let time slip through our fingers. Instead, let's use it to climb the rope to our goals, our purpose, and ultimately to God's destiny for our lives.

GET READY

1. Go through the following Time Exercise. Make sure you have completed your purpose, values, and goals first, so that they tie into your time decisions.

2. Have your parents or a friend hold you accountable for the use of your time. Go over the Time Exercise with them.

TIME EXERCISE

To use your time most wisely, take these steps.

1. To observe accurately how you live, fill out the Time Log on page 114 for one week. It will help you know with accuracy where your time is going now. You will be surprised!

2. To make every minute count, fill out the Ideal Schedule on page 115. The Ideal Schedule should reflect your monthly goals.

Fill in the Ideal Schedule by looking back over your monthly goals. Place each monthly goal into the schedule or otherwise you are not purposefully pursuing that goal.

For example, if one of my One Year Goals is "To spend time alone with God daily" and my One Month Goal is "To spend thirty minutes in prayer and Bible study every day," then I fill that in on my calendar for thirty minutes every day.

Fill in the entire schedule. That way you plan your time rather than others planning it for you. That does not mean you are selfish or exclude other people. But it indicates that you have a prepared strategy for making every minute count with God, others, and yourself.

3. To control the time, order a calendar/planning system at an office supply store. One such option is the Student Daymaker, which can be ordered from

Customer Services
1-800-458-2772
or fax (615) 251-5933

You need the proper tools for planning in the same way you need a lawnmower for cutting the yard. A tool like the Daytimer gives an opportunity to record your schedules and notes in one place and have it before you every day. This tool is critical when you put your monthly goals into your schedule.

When your calendar arrives, go through each day of the month putting in your Ideal Schedule each week. Then make certain that every monthly goal is either on the schedule or on your daily To Do list.

To make sure you are doing first things first, you should prioritize the To Do list. At the end of the day, if you have completed only your first priority, you can rest assured you have done the most important thing.

As you turn these steps into habits, you build confidence each day that you are accomplishing your goals, your purpose, and ultimately your destiny.

DAILY TIME LOG

	Sunday	Monday	Tuesday	Wednesday	Thursday	Friday	Saturday
6:00							
6:30							
7:00							
7:30							
8:00							
8:30							
9:00							
9:30							
10:00							
10:30							
11:00							
11:30							
12:00							
12:30							
1:00							
1:30							
2:00							
2:30							
3:00							
3:30							
4:00							
4:30							
5:00							
5:30							
6:00							
6:30							
7:00							
7:30							
8:00							
8:30							
9:00							
9:30							
10:00							
10:30							
11:00							
11:30							

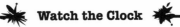
IDEAL TIME SCHEDULE

	Sunday	Monday	Tuesday	Wednesday	Thursday	Friday	Saturday
6:00							
6:30							
7:00							
7:30							
8:00							
8:30							
9:00							
9:30							
10:00							
10:30							
11:00							
11:30							
12:00							
12:30							
1:00							
1:30							
2:00							
2:30							
3:00							
3:30							
4:00							
4:30							
5:00							
5:30							
6:00							
6:30							
7:00							
7:30							
8:00							
8:30							
9:00							
9:30							
10:00							
10:30							
11:00							
11:30							

Warp and Weft 'Em

What decisions do you need to make, and how do you make them?

Marcia weaves. When she explained how she weaves, I was totally fascinated. "I hold in my hand many strands of yarn. Then I place those longer strands on the warp. They will run the length of the fabric. When I place in other threads that run the other direction, it is called the weft. As they cross over and under, they give the fabric color and design. I can put in strong threads or weak ones. I can weave it tightly or loosely. Each of those decisions determines what the fabric will look like when I have finished."

MAKING DECISIONS PARALLELS MARCIA'S weaving. We hold the yarn of our decisions in our hands. When we make a decision, it is like placing the strands of yarn on the loom. Those decisions warp and weft to become the fabric of our lives.

As Marcia continued teaching me about weaving, she said, "In order to know what the final product will look like, I must have a 'draft.' A draft is the formula for making the pattern. Then using the treadle, the pedal that makes the pattern, and the headle—the gadget that picks up the threads—I weave the fabric to match the pattern."

Decisions do not stand alone. Rather, they are woven into the very fabric of our lives. When we understand that the decisions we make make us, we see not only the significance of every decision we make, but also the value of a "draft," a plan for our decision making.

From Philippians 2:3–13 let's develop the acrostic **DECIDE** as our "draft."

DISCERN OUR ATTITUDE

The initial "fork in the road" on any decision is our attitude.

According to the apostle Paul in Philippians 2:3–5, what are our two attitude options?

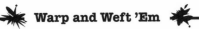
1. _____

2. _____

We can ask ourselves two questions to discern our attitude.

1. Am I making this decision to get what I want? *A selfish attitude.*

2. Am I making this decision to do what Jesus wants even if I don't get what I want? *A servant attitude.*

I want to buy a car. What is the first step I take in making that decision? Not cost, model, or color, but motive, attitude. Why am I buying a car?

Decisive question: Will this decision serve me or serve Christ?

EXALT JESUS AS THE LORD

Next, we want Jesus to rule over every detail of the decision-making process.

How did that work in Jesus' own life in His relationship with His Father, according to Philippians 2:6–11?

_____

_____

_____

Living under Jesus' lordship means He will show us what He desires and will guide us to make the decision wisely.

Without factoring Jesus into the car decision, describe the car you would buy:

_____

_____

_____

How would your friends react?

_____

_____

How would you pay for it?

_____

_____

It is very easy to get ahead of ourselves in the decision-making process. We must stop and remember Proverbs 16:9: "We should make plans—counting on God to direct us" (TLB).

Bottom line: Is this decision based on what Jesus desires? Who knows, He may want to give you a car! Or He may want you to buy a used one. Or He may want to protect you from buying a certain one.

I had the check ready to buy the car. But I told the Lord: "If for any reason You don't want us to have this, show me and I won't buy it." When I took it to my mechanic to check it out, he discovered that it had been in a severe wreck that had bent the frame! We didn't get that car! Submitting that decision to the Lord saved us mega-hassles and untold dollars.

Decisive question: Is this decision based on what Jesus desires?

CHOOSE TO OBEY

Our next logical step is to obey what God tells us to do.

How does the apostle Paul present that challenge in Philippians 2:12?

_____

_____

_____

To grasp the word *obeyed,* picture someone in a house who hears a rap at the door. That person goes to the door and opens it. He responds. She obeys. Done often enough that becomes a habit, a lifestyle. If we choose to obey God, then with each decision it becomes easier and easier until obedience becomes a lifestyle.

In your opinion what would it mean to you to obey Christ in buying a car?

_____

_____

Obedience removes the possibility of making a decision based on

- impulse
- impatience
- feelings
- frustrations
- disappointment

- people's expectations
- pressure

We were willing not to buy and walk if that is what the Lord had in mind.

We had to start back at square one after not getting the wrecked car. We felt frustrated and disappointed. The pressure was building to buy because our mechanic wanted promised that our old car was not long for this world. What I to say was, "Lord, I want a car now!" But instead I said, "Lord, I choose to obey so I can have your exact plan for the car."

By the simple statement "I choose to obey," we put ourselves in position to make a wise decision.

Decisive question: Am I choosing to obey?

IMPLEMENT THE STEPS

The next step in making a decision is to work through the decision-making process using the **STEPS** approach.

What do you think "continue to work out your own salvation" (Philippians 2:12) has to do with decision making?

_____

_____

_____

Paul had this in mind: to work out every detailed decision to the finish. This verse is not about earning our salvation by works; rather it refers to the ongoing process of making Christlike decisions once we have salvation.

We make those decisions by working through a practical, five-step process. We can use this process to buy a car, decide which cereal to eat for breakfast, decide who to marry, or any other decision we make.[1]

- **S**ee *the goal clearly.* Focus on your goal.

Ask the Lord to make the goal clear based on His promise in Proverbs 2:6: "For the LORD gives wisdom, and from his mouth come knowledge and understanding."

_____

_____

_____

In order to avoid confusion later, write down your goal.

- **T**ake in the facts. Thoroughly analyze the situation, getting all the facts before you. Ask the "who, what, where, when, why" questions.

Seriously consider the challenge of Proverbs 18:13: "What a shame —yes, how stupid!—to decide before knowing the facts!" (TLB).

So you will have a firm grip on the facts, write them down.

- **E**valuate the alternatives. Explore all of the creative alternatives.

The writer of Proverbs encourages this openness in Proverbs 18:15: "The intelligent man is always open to new ideas. In fact, he looks for them" (TLB).

Outline all of the possible alternatives.

- **P**roject strengths and weaknesses. Use the **SWOT** approach.

  Strengths. What are the strengths about this alternative?

  Weaknesses. What are the weaknesses about this alternative?

  Opportunities. What opportunities does this provide for the future?

  Threats. What threats does this create for the future?

Write out the strengths, weaknesses, opportunities and threats for each alternative.

- **S**elect the best alternative. Prayerfully select the alternative that emerges as the best one.

The Lord will direct you according to His promise in Proverbs 3:5–6: "Trust in the LORD with all your heart and lean not on your own understanding; in all your ways acknowledge him, and he will make your paths straight."

We set aside all day Saturday to go through these steps. We focused on the kind of car we needed. Then we went to several dealers to get the facts, taking lots of notes. We narrowed it down to two dealers who had the same car. Before we decided we put one car on one page and the other on another page, going through strengths and weaknesses. At that point the decision was easy. We got a much newer, nicer car than we had ever imagined!

Decisive question: Am I using **STEPS** to think through this decision?

Delight in the Decision

We can relax with the confidence that we have made the best possible decision. Check out Philippians 2:13 to find out why.

_____

_____

_____

At this point we experience the fulfillment of His promise in Psalm 37:4: "Delight yourself in the LORD and he will give you the desires of your heart."

> When, finally, we bought our car, we were delighted. We trusted the Lord through these steps. He not only protected us from "the wreck"; He provided His very best for us. In fact, the car He provided was so good we wondered if the dealer lost money on us!

Decisive question: Am I enjoying this decision?

Evaluate with Tests

Let's say we follow this process, but the decision is still not clear. Or we make what appears to be an unwise decision.

Our destiny does not hinge on making every decision correctly. We will make mistakes. God uses even our wrong decisions in the process of working out His salvation in us. He weaves that dark yarn into the fabric to make the overall design more beautiful. We learn and grow from the experience.

But how can we check our decision to evaluate if it is the right one?

> F. B. Meyer told about a large ship that navigated into a narrow harbor at night. The captain could easily run the ship aground, but he never did. He always got the ship into the harbor. Asked how he did it, he replied that when the five lights in the harbor lined up in a straight line, then he knew he could turn the ship into the channel.

These five lights will help us evaluate our decisions.

1. *The communication test.* Have we talked to God seriously about this decision. *Have I listened intently to hear His answer?*

2. *The conscience test.* With the Holy Spirit living in us as our Counselor, He will show us the rightness or wrongness of the decision. *Does my conscience confirm this decision?*

3. *The conviction test.* God will confirm the decision with a promise from His Word. It won't be just a nice verse, but a powerful promise that gives us confidence that this is the right decision. *Do I have a promise from God?*

4. *The counselor test.* Test the validity of the decision through the affirmation of people whose opinions we respect—parents, boss, or close friends. *Have those I respect confirmed the decision?*

5. *The calmness test.* We can picture ourselves carrying out the decision. Sleep on it. If the peace of Christ rules in your heart (Colossians 3:15) the next day, then move ahead. If not, reevaluate. *Do I have peace about the decision?*

When all five of these line up, you have thoroughly evaluated your decision and can move forward with even greater confidence. *Decisive question:* Have I thoroughly evaluated this decision? *You make your decisions, then your decisions make you!*

> Every time you make a choice, you are turning the central part of you that chooses into something a little different from what it was before. And taking your life as a whole with all of your innumerable choices, all your life long you are slowly turning this central thing either into a heavenly creature or a hellish creature. C. S. Lewis[2]

> When Marcia, my friend, finishes weaving, she has a beautiful fabric, each piece unique according to the draft she set up. When you have placed the yarn of your decisions on God's loom, you can have confidence that God is weaving every decision according to His draft, His perfect plan for you.

GET READY

Pick one major decision you face now. Use the **DECIDE** approach to make that decision. Process that through the sheet on the next page. Carry one with you so you can refer to it in the decisions you make.

DECIDE

The Decision:

_____

_____

Discern Your Attitude. Will this decision serve me or serve Christ?
Exalt Jesus as Lord. Is this decision based on what Jesus desires?
Choose to Obey. Am I choosing to obey?
Implement the **STEPS** Am I using **STEPS** to think through the decision?

      See the goal clearly.
      Take in the facts.
      Evaluate the alternatives.
      Project strengths and weaknesses.
      Select the best alternative.

Delight in the decision. Am I enjoying this decision?
Evaluate with tests. Have I thoroughly evaluated this decision?

      Communication test (listen intently)
      Conscience test (Holy Spirit confirmation)
      Conviction test (promise from God)
      Counselor test (someone I respect)
      Calmness test (peace)

DECIDE

The Decision: _____
Discern Your Attitude. Will this decision serve me or serve Christ?
Exalt Jesus as Lord. Is this decision based on what Jesus desires?
Choose to Obey. Am I choosing to obey?
Implement the **STEPS** Am I using **STEPS** to think through the decision?
    See the goal clearly.
    Take in the facts .
    Evaluate the alternatives.
    Project strengths and weaknesses.
    Select the best alternative.
Delight in the decision. Am I enjoying this decision?
Evaluate with tests. Have I thoroughly evaluated this decision?
    Communication test (listen intently)
    Conscience test (Holy Spirit confirmation)
    Conviction test (promise from God)
    Counselor test (someone I respect)
    Calmness test (peace)

chapter 14

Put Together "The Visible Man"

What is integrity, and how do you pursue it?

On those days when nothing else would keep the kids attention, my wife would drag out "The Visible Man." Its description: "An exciting dimensional model of the human body." Open the box and out pops the skull, sternum, ribs, liver, heart, stomach, and intestines. In addition it was equipped with ears, fibula, tibia . . . you get the idea. The "exciting" part of "The Visible Man" was that someone got to put these parts together.

NOW THAT WE HAVE OPENED THE BOX and looked at the various aspects of discovering our destiny, we need to put all of the pieces together, to integrate them, so we can see the whole picture.

The word *integrity* gets tossed around a lot. But these days who knows what it means? Integrity comes from the math word *integer,* a whole—all of the fractions add up to a whole number. Webster's Dictionary defines integrity as "(1) the quality or state of being complete; unbroken; whole; (2) unimpaired; perfect condition; sound; (3) sound moral principles; upright; honest; sincere."

Conclusion: a person with integrity is integrated; all parts of his or her life add up to the whole.

SHAPE UP!

In God's amazing creativity He made each one of us vastly different from all others. Our job is to shape up: to discover how to take all of these different parts and shape them into our unique destiny.

How does Job affirm that in Job 10:8?

_____

_____

_____

What illustration does Paul use in Romans 9:20–21?

_____

_____

_____

• What is his point?

_____

_____

_____

That "unique shape" manifests itself in a variety of individuals throughout the Bible.

Joseph

- The gift of a multicolored coat showed the love of his father.
- Being thrown in a pit and sold as a slave expressed the hatred of his brothers.
- Resisting the sexual advances of Potiphar's wife deepened his convictions.
- Years in prison for doing nothing wrong built his character.
- His rise to be an official of Egypt revealed his leadership ability.

Years later, reflecting on what his brothers had done, Joseph could see how God had shaped him. What perspective did he have? (Genesis 50:20)

_____

_____

_____

God shaped him into a man capable of saving not only his family but his nation.

Moses
- A man of privilege raised in Pharoah's household for forty years.
- A man God sent into the desert for forty years.
- God spoke to Moses in a burning bush.

✳ When Moses complained that he had nothing to offer, what did the Lord say to him in Exodus 4:10–12?

_____

_____

_____

God shaped him uniquely to lead the Israelites out of Egypt.

David
- The youngest son, he was sent by his dad to tend the sheep while his brothers went to war.
- In the fields with the sheep, he experienced God's presence and power.
- God anointed him to be king at an early age.
- A fierce warrior, he killed Goliath.
- Chased by madman King Saul, David lived in caves for several years.

✳ In all of these experiences, what one main quality did God look for to shape David's life (1 Samuel 13:14)?

_____

_____

_____

Later God used him to shape the destiny of a nation.

Esther
- A devout Jew, she was also a beautiful woman.
- She caught the eye of the king and became queen.
- As queen she found herself in the unusual position of being the only person who could appeal to the king not to destroy her people.

What profound challenge did her Uncle Mordecai give her in Esther 4:14?

_____

_____

_____

Esther's grace under pressure shaped her destiny and that of the entire Jewish nation.

Job

- Early in his life he discovered success in all he did.
- Bombarded with Satan's entire arsenal, everything around him fell apart.
- He lost his work, friends, possessions, family, and health.

In spite of it all, Job refused to toss in the towel. In Job 27:5 he tells us what kept him going?

_____

_____

_____

His trust in God's unique shape for him led him to live out his unique destiny.

Up, Up, and Away!

No less than any of these famous Bible characters, God has uniquely shaped each of us to achieve His destiny for us. But we short-circuit that when we think negatively:

- "God could never use me like that."
- "My life can't make much difference."
- "Only the 'rich and the famous' influence the world."

Yet if we faithfully pursue our destiny, God will use our humble lives to make a difference for His purposes.

How can man now jet around the world and even fly to the moon? Air and space travel had a humble beginning. In 1670, an Italian monk, Francesco de Lana, developed a vacuum balloon that supported a cart equipped with oars and a sail. His flight experiment failed because he overlooked the phenomenon of atmospheric pressure, which crushed the balloon. Years later the Montgolfier brothers, inspired by Francesco de Lana and watching wood chips float over a fire, lifted a balloon six thousand feet in the air. They repeated the experiment for King Louis XVI with a sheep, rooster, and duck as the balloon's passengers. From that Henri Giffard flew a dirigible powered by a steam engine and propeller. Then the Wright brothers flew at Kitty Hawk . . . and now people explore space.

Humble beginnings, seemingly insignificant events, mostly unknown individuals laid the foundation for the next big step. Certainly they even doubted themselves at times. They must have asked the question: "Can it be done?" But they pursued their hopes and dreams, their unique destiny, and did it.[1]

When we pursue God's unique destiny, we can change the question, "Can it be done?" into a statement, "It can be done!"

ALL PUT TOGETHER

In conclusion, we want to add all the fractions of our lives discovered in this book. When we do, we will be 80 percent of the distance in knowing our destiny. The other 20 percent, which has to do with whether or not we marry, who our marriage partner might be, and what our careers will look like, become clear as we pursue the 80 percent. Many people wake up at forty or fifty years old and realize that they have never put together the 80 percent. Many are frustrated. Others are devastated. But you have the privilege of putting your life together early.

To bring us full circle, Jesus Christ is the one who puts all of the various parts together to make us complete (Colossians 2:10). No one else can do it. In Him all the parts come together into the whole. Around Him we have developed a "life plan" that we can live by every day for the rest of our lives. It has answered and will continue to answer these questions:

1. What will be the center of my life?
   (Who or what am I going to live for?)

2. What will be the character of my life?
   (Who am I going to be?)

3. What will be the contribution of my life?
   (What strengths do I have?)

4. What will be the communication of my life?
(What will God say to the world through me?) [2]

As we continue to discover the various aspects of who we are, then put them into action in our lives, God will use us. The more we act on what we have learned, the more we will be integrated into a whole person conformed more and more into the image of Jesus Christ. Then we will positively influence the world for Christ through our own unique destiny!

GET READY

1. Evaluate how integrated you are by filling in the Integrity Questions at the end of the chapter.

2. Complete the picture of who you are by writing your summary answers to the Total Picture which follows.

3. Keep it in your Bible or a notebook as a constant reminder of who you are, where you are going, and how you are going to get there.

4. Decide how to plug what you have learned into a place to serve. Show the Total Picture to your parents or youth leader and ask their suggestions.

PLUGGED IN IDEAS:

1. Serve in the youth ministry at your church using what you have learned about yourself.

2. Pray for and care for friends on your campus who need Christ. Use what you have learned about yourself to do that.

3. Using your new discoveries, teach the younger children in your church.

4. Disciple some younger students at your school or in your youth group, using what you have learned about yourself.

5. Work as a counselor at a camp in the summer applying what you have learned to that situation.

6. Go on a mission trip.

INTEGRITY QUESTIONS

Rank where you are on a scale of 1–10 (1=lowest, 10-highest).

Personality—Am I using what I know about my personality to maximize my strengths and minimize my weaknesses?

   1   2   3   4   5   6   7   8   9   10

Spiritual gifts—Am I using my spiritual gifts in a specific ministry?

   1   2   3   4   5   6   7   8   9   10

Abilities—Am I using my abilities and experiences to build the kingdom of God?

   1   2   3   4   5   6   7   8   9   10

Motives—Am I motivated toward investing my life in God's plans and purposes?

   1   2   3   4   5   6   7   8   9   10

Purpose—Do I know my purpose and am I pursuing it?

   1   2   3   4   5   6   7   8   9   10

Values—Are my values determining my behavior?

   1   2   3   4   5   6   7   8   9   10

Goals—Am I pursuing my long- and short-term goals?

   1   2   3   4   5   6   7   8   9   10

Time—Am I using my time to pursue God's purpose and goals for my life?

   1   2   3   4   5   6   7   8   9   10

Decisions—Am I making daily decisions that keep me in line with God's plan for me?

   1   2   3   4   5   6   7   8   9   10

From the evaluation take the three lowest scores and decide what you need to do to integrate those more into your daily life.

1. _____

2. _____

3. _____

THE TOTAL PICTURE

Put together the total picture of who you are, where you are going, and how you are going to get there. In order to do this you may need to review the "Get Ready" section in each of the chapters. Make your picture as clear and concise as you possibly can.

My destiny: _____

My purpose: _____

My personality: _____

My abilities and experiences:

    1. _____

    2. _____

    3. _____

    4. _____

    5. _____

My values:

    1. _____

    2. _____

    3. _____

    4. _____

    5. _____

    6. _____

My motivation:

    1. _____

    2. _____

    3. _____

    4. _____

    5. _____

My goals:

    1. _____

    2. _____

    3. _____

    4. _____

    5. _____

My time plan: _____

My decisions (ones to make in light of what I discovered):

    1. _____

    2. _____

    3. _____

My destination: _____

THE TOTAL PICTURE

My destiny: _____

My purpose:

_____

My personality:

_____

My values:

_____
_____
_____
_____
_____
_____

My abilities &
experience:

_____
_____
_____
_____
_____
_____

My goals:

_____
_____
_____
_____
_____
_____

My motivation:

_____
_____
_____
_____
_____
_____

My big decisions:

_____
_____
_____
_____

My time plan:

_____
_____

My destination: _____ _____

Notes

Chapter 2

1. William Barclay, "The Letter to the Galatians and Ephesians," *The Daily Study Bible,* 88–89.

Chapter 3

1. Peter Marshall Jr. and David Manuel, *The Light and the Glory* (Old Tappan, N. J.: Fleming H. Revell Co., 1977).

Chapter 4

1. Larry Crabb, *Inside Out* (Colorado Springs, Colo.: NavPress, 1988), 80–81.

Chapter 5

1. Tim LaHaye, *Spirit-Controlled Temperament* (Wheaton, Ill.: Tyndale House, 1966), 10.
2. Information on these personality types came from a variety of sources including Tim LaHaye, *Spirit-Controlled Temperament;* Fred and Florence Littauer, "Personality Plus" (Forrest and Nancy Mobley, "Marriage Lifelines" notebook based on the DISC test (Tallassee, Ala.:) and my personal observations.
3. The instructions, test, and scoring sheet were developed for me by Bill Kallenburg of Student Leadership Development (Avondale, Ga.).

Chapter 7

1. "Discovering My S.H.A.P.E. for Ministry" (Ft. Worth, Texas: Hope Baptist Church), 37.
2. Dennis Rainey, *Soapbox* newsletter (Little Rock, Ark., 1986).
3. The Abilities Survey is adapted from an abilities test in "Discovering My S.H.A.P.E. for Ministry," 35–36.

Chapter 8

1. Alan Loy McGinnis, *Bringing Out the Best in People* (Minneapolis, Minn.: Augsburg, 1985), 15.

Chapter 9

1. Quoted from Billy Graham, *World Aflame* (Garden City, N. Y.: Doubleday, 1965), 64.
2. Walt Henriksen, *Disciples Are Made Not Born* (Wheaton, Ill.: Scripture Press, 1988), 150.
3. Mack R. Douglas, *How to Make a Habit of Succeeding* (Grand Rapids: Zondervan Publishing, 1966), 19.
4. Some of the questions were adapted from material by Bobb Biehl of Master Planning Associates, P.O. Box 6128, Laguna Niguel, CA 72677.

Chapter 10

1. Charles Hobbs, "Your Time and Your Life" tape series and workbook, Charles R. Hobbs Corporation (7300 N. Lehigh Ave., Chicago, IL 60648).
2. T. B. Maston and William Pinson Jr., *Right from Wrong?* (Nashville: Broadman Press, 1971), 15–20.

Chapter 11

1. Mike Philips, *Getting More Done in Less Time* (Minneapolis, Minn.: Bethany House Publishers, 1982), 55.
2. Wilberta L. Chinn, *Personal Goal Setting for a Purposeful and Fulfilled Life* (Whittier, Calif.: Peacock Enterprises, 1984).
3. Glenn Bland, *Success! The Glenn Bland Method* (Wheaton, Ill.: Tyndale, 1972), 44.

Chapter 12

1. Edward R. Dayton and Ted W. Engstrom, *Strategy for Living* (Oxnard, Calif.: Gospel Light Publishing, 1976).
2. The Charles Hobbs "Your Time and Your Life" tape series (Chicago, Ill.: Nightingale-Conant Corporation), and Edward R. Dayton, *Tools for Time Management* (Grand Rapids: Zondervan Publishing House), 176.
3. Quoted in Dayton and Engstrom, *Strategy for Living,* 177.
4. Mike Philips, *Getting More Done in Less Time* (Minneapolis, Minn.: Bethany House Publishers), 35.
5. Les Christie, *Getting a Grip on Time Management* (Wheaton, Ill.: Victor Books, 1984), 32.
6. Quoted in Christie, 32.

Chapter 13

1. Myron Rush, *Management: A Biblical Approach* (Wheaton, Ill.: Victor Books, 1983), 102–106.
2. C. S. Lewis, *Christian Behavior* (New York: MacMillen, 1943), 23.

Chapter 14

1. Taken from a newsletter published by Bill Kallenberg.
2. Rick Warren and Tom Patterson, "Defining Your Life Mission" tape (Authentic Leadership Inc., 550 Old Orchard, Holland, MI 49423).